D1245496

<u>Even</u> <u>more</u> recipes from the backs of boxes, bottles, cans and jars

Books by Ceil Dyer include:

The After-Work Entertaining Cookbook
Carter Family Favorites Cookbook
The Chopped, Minced and Ground Meat Cookbook
Coffee Cookery
The Eat to Lose Cookbook
Freezer to Oven to Table
Plan-Ahead Cookbook
Wok Cookery
Best Recipes from the Backs of Boxes, Bottles,
    Cans and Jars
More Recipes from the Backs of Boxes, Bottles,
    Cans and Jars

<u>Even</u> <u>more</u> recipes from the backs of boxes, bottles, cans and jars

by Ceil Dyer

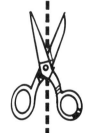

McGraw-Hill Book Company

New York   St. Louis   San Francisco
Toronto   Hamburg   Mexico

1 2 3 4 5 6 7 8 F G F G 8 7 6 5 4 3 2

ISBN 0-07-018558-1 {H.C.}
ISBN 0-07-018559-X {PBK.}

LIBRARY OF CONGRESS CATALOGING IN PUBLICATION DATA

Dyer, Ceil.
Even more recipes from the backs of boxes,
bottles, cans, and jars.
1. Cookery.   I. Title.
TX715.D97735   641.5   81-17144
ISBN 0-07-018558-1   AACR2
ISBN 0-07-018559-X (Pbk)

Contents

We wish to thank the following for permission to use these recipes:

Diamond Walnut Growers, Inc.
Sunsweet Growers, Inc.
Sun-Maid Growers of California
Libby, McNeill & Libby, Inc.
C. F. Mueller Company
Oscar Mayer & Company
Pacific Pearl Seafoods
Land O Lakes, Inc.
Welch Foods, Inc.
Hunt-Wesson Kitchens
Hillshire Farm
The Dannon Company
Standard Brands, Inc.
Kikkoman International, Inc.
Ralston Purina Company
Sunkist Growers, Inc.
Nabisco, Inc.
McIlhenny Company
International Multifoods
The Pillsbury Company
Best Foods, a Division of CPC
 International, Inc.
Gerber Products Company
Thomas J. Lipton, Inc.
Pompeian, Inc.
California Almond Growers
 Exchange

Universal Foods Corporation
Forst Von Taaffe
Pet, Inc.
Armour and Company
The Nestlé Company
Borden, Inc.
The R. T. French Company
Kraft, Inc.
General Mills, Inc.
W. A. Taylor
Pepperidge Farm, Inc.
General Foods Corp.
Purity Cheese Company
Castle & Cooke Foods, a Division of
 Castle & Cooke, Inc.
The Procter & Gamble Company
Delmarva Poultry Industry, Inc.
Kellogg Company
Heublein
Stokely–Van Camp, Inc.
Campbell Soup Company
William J. Underwood Company
Holland House Brands Company
Argo-Kingsford Company

Introduction

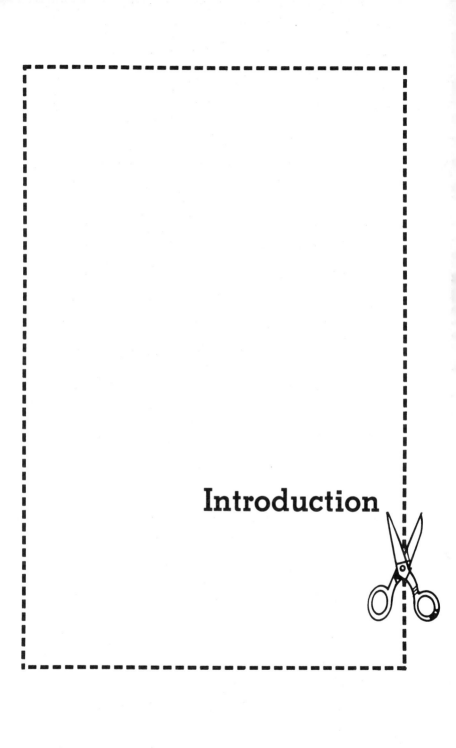

Why a third book of Best Recipes? To expand your culinary horizons. This newest collection of "tried and trues" will do just that, with recipes you'll find downright irresistible.

As in Book I and Book II each recipe here is from a well-known food company. Each was tested and retested, analyzed, criticized and then retested again until it was declared so delicious, so truly good it could be put in a company booklet, used in a national ad or put on a label or box of the company's product and shipped with confidence across the country for millions of Americans to buy, cook, eat and love.

For this book I asked each company to go through their permanent files (files made up of their most-requested consumer favorites) and select from these top-ranking recipes what they themselves felt were the all-time best results of their test kitchen's efforts. In other words I asked for the best of their best.

My harvest: a collection of recipes I call "plus extras"; extra great tasting, exceptionally appetizing, especially easy to prepare, pleasantly thrifty and nutritious—or just sinfully "forget-the-calories" good.

I think you will find this book satisfying in its variety;

with entrée and side dishes, salads and soups ranging from light luncheon fare to almost total meals that satisfy a big hunger. There's a new category chapter: "Appetizers, Snacks, Noshes and Such," that fits right into the more casual way we live these days. It starts with "go withs" for your favorite beverage, but then goes on to double-quick-to-make Tex-Mex specials, hot and cold sandwiches, pizzas, fondues and more; all substitute nicely (and nutritionally) for more formal meals. There's a chapter on honest, fragrant home-baked breads (was there ever anything better?), and one completely devoted to America's favorite pies. You'll find a chapter of the best-you-ever-ate cakes and other fabulous desserts and a sweet last chapter with treats to please everyone from age five (or less) to ninety-five (or more). Three (and in some cases four) generations of very experienced cooks have worked hard to produce these recipes and whether your taste runs to fine gourmet food or hearty, simple dishes, you are going to enjoy every recipe you try from these pages, every dish that you cook and undoubtedly will cook and enjoy many times again. After all, there's a reason a recipe withstands the test of time and that reason is just plain, old-fashioned good taste.

Whether it's a nosh or a snack, a meal or a sweet, "here's good cooking" to you and yours.

1.

Appetizers,
Snacks,
Noshes and Such

These days "cook's in the kitchen while madam awaits dinner" is a dreamy world we may read about but will rarely, if ever, see again. I can remember those good old days (yes, I am that old) and believe me they weren't all that good. Though the average middle-income family did indeed have hired help, either part- or full-time, life was too rigid, too formal, and there were too many "unbreakable" rules for both adults and children alike. As for the food, it was good, but menus were not as interesting or varied as they are now, service was stiff and rarely was a meal really fun—certainly not for the hired cook. Thank goodness she's gone. I miss her not in the least. Now I cook it *my* way and serve it when and how *I* prefer. When I want to see my friends, but don't have time to prepare a party menu, I ask them over for drinks and appetizers or just coffee and "maybe a nosh." When I don't want to cook or eat out I simply put together a great-tasting snack and enjoy it twice as much as a formal meal no matter how nicely served. In fact, like most people today, I've found that casual eating and entertaining has become a part of my less rigid, more enjoyable and rule-free life.

This chapter is made up of what I call "casual" food.

Easy to fix, fun to eat food—to serve with drinks, to take on a picnic, to put on a tray and serve out on the terrace, in the garden or in front of the TV in the den or the playroom. No formal service is needed or wanted. This is "finger" food or food that requires no more than a fork to enjoy.

Each recipe is, of course, from the test kitchens of a famous food company. Quite a few were put on the label or box any number of years ago, but they all fit like a hand in a glove into this new grouping of versatile meals. Less effort to fix than a trip to a fast foods take-out window and twice as good, they are the kind of great tasting things just about everyone likes; just what's wanted when the cook (that's you) takes the night off; just what's needed when friends drop by—and just right too when there's only "family" and all that's wanted is something easy to cook but flavorful and fun." Nothing heavy, you know, just a snack."

These quickies from Hillshire Farms®—all for sausage fans in a hurry for something really good.

Piggy Wraps

1 package Hillshire Farm® Sausage
1 package refrigerated crescent dough

Cut Sausage into desired shapes. Wrap in dough. Bake at 400°F. for 5 minutes or until golden brown. May be frozen.

Sweet and Saucy

Equal parts currant jelly and catsup
1 package Hillshire Farm® Sausage, cut up

Heat jelly and catsup in saucepan. Add bite-size pieces of Sausage and heat until Sausage is hot. Serve with toothpicks.

Italian Nachos

1 package Hillshire Farm® Italian Smoked Sausage
1 bag tortilla chips
Monterey Jack or taco-flavored cheese
Sour cream for garnish (optional)

Place thinly sliced Sausage on tortilla chips. Top with cheese and broil until cheese melts. If desired, garnish with sour cream.

Pickled Shrimp

Charleston, South Carolina, takes credit for "inventing" Pickled Shrimp but you can thank the French® Company for this easy version.

1 to 1½ pounds cooked, shelled and
  deveined medium or large shrimp
2 medium-size onions, thinly sliced and
  rings separated
16 to 20 bay leaves
1 to 1½ cups Piquant French Dressing (below)
  Crackers

In medium-size bowl arrange alternate layers of shrimp, onion rings and bay leaves. Pour dressing over the top, pressing down so top layer is covered. Let stand in refrigerator at least 24 hours to blend flavors. Serve as an hors d'oeuvre on crackers, as a cocktail or in a salad.

Piquant French Dressing

1 tsp. Colman's® (dry)   1½ tsps. salt
  Mustard   1 tsp. sugar
1 tsp. water   1 tsp. paprika
1½ cups oil   ¼ tsp. cayenne pepper
⅔ cup vinegar
1 Tbs. French's®
  Worcestershire Sauce

Mix mustard with water and let stand 10 minutes to develop flavor. Combine all ingredients in a jar. Cover tightly and shake.

Crab Ball Hors d'Oeuvre

This outstanding recipe appeared in national magazine advertising a couple of years ago from Wakefield® Snow Crabmeat and it's become a great favorite. Walnuts can be used instead of pecans.

1 6-oz. package
  Wakefield® Snow
  Crabmeat
1 8-oz. package cream
  cheese, softened

2 tsps. chopped chives
¼ tsp. garlic powder
¼ tsp. salt
½ cup chopped pecans

Thaw and drain crabmeat. Blend softened cream cheese, chives, garlic powder and salt. Fold in crabmeat. Shape into log or ball. Roll in pecans. Serve with crackers or fresh vegetables.

Spinach Beef Dip

Armour's® test kitchen director tells me that this label recipe was the first dip to use thawed but uncooked spinach as an ingredient. It's terrific; so easy to make ahead and store in your refrigerator until party time, and it tastes even better for waiting.

1 10-oz. package frozen chopped spinach,
  thawed and drained
1 8-oz. package cream cheese, softened
1 cup mayonnaise
½ cup chopped green onions
1 Tbs. dillweed
1 2½-oz. jar Armour® Star Sliced Dried Beef,
  rinsed and chopped
  Assorted crackers

Combine spinach, cream cheese, mayonnaise, green onions and dillweed in container of electric blender; process on high speed 1 to 2 minutes or until smooth and creamy. Fold in Dried Beef. Chill. Serve with crackers. Makes 3 cups.

Make-Ahead Ham & Mushroom Paté

This recipe from the label of Underwood® Deviled Ham was one of their most popular. It's well worth keeping in your permanent file. Easy to make and very special in flavor.

 1 Tbs. butter or margarine
¼ lb. coarsely chopped fresh
   mushrooms
 2 4½-oz. cans Underwood®
   Deviled Ham
 1 3-oz. package cream
   cheese, softened
¼ tsp. ground thyme
   Party bread slices

Day before:
Melt butter in a skillet and sauté mushrooms over medium heat until tender. Combine Deviled Ham, cream cheese and thyme; blend well. Stir in sautéed mushrooms. Cover and chill overnight. Serve on party bread slices. Makes 1¾ cups paté.

Cheesy Corn Spread

Whole kernel corn is the surprise ingredient in this recipe. It's a favorite with the home-economists at the Green Giant® test kitchens and with me, too—as well as with literally hundreds of other good cooks.

12 oz. (3 cups) shredded sharp Cheddar cheese	½ tsp. salt
½ cup dairy sour cream	1 12-oz. can Green Giant® Mexicorn Golden Whole Kernel Corn with Sweet Peppers, drained
½ cup salad dressing or mayonnaise	
¼ cup finely chopped onion	

Bring cheese to room temperature. In large bowl, crumble cheese with fork or blend with mixer to form small bits. Mix in remaining ingredients, except corn, until well blended. Stir in corn. Cover; chill several hours or overnight. Can be stored in the refrigerator up to 1 week. Serve with raw vegetables or crackers. Makes 3½ cups.

Tropical Fruit Nibbles

The Almond Growers test kitchens say serve this lovely fruit with wooden picks . . . and a tropical drink I hope?

¼ cup light rum
¼ cup orange juice
 1 tsp. French's® Almond Extract or Coconut
  Flavor
  Melon balls, pineapple chunks, grapes, or
  other fresh fruit.

Combine rum, orange juice and extract; pour over fruit and refrigerate 30 minutes. Serve with wooden picks.

Alaska Shrimp Quiche

Wakefield® test-kitchen cooks suggest this deluxe quiche for a buffet supper or cocktail party.

1 6-oz. package	1 4-oz. can sliced
Wakefield® Shrimp	mushrooms, drained
1 9-inch pie shell	1 tsp. chopped chives
4 eggs	Dash pepper
1 cup half-and-half	Dash nutmeg
½ tsp. salt	½ cup grated Swiss cheese

Thaw and drain Shrimp well. Beat together the eggs, half-and-half and seasonings. Place mushrooms and shrimp in bottom of pie shell. Sprinkle with cheese. Add egg mixture and bake at 375°F. for 35 to 40 minutes or until center is firm. To prepare quiche ahead, bake 10 minutes less than directed; cool, then wrap and freeze. When ready to use, unwrap and bake at 325°F. for 25 minutes.

Alternate suggestions: For a delicious Alaska Crab Quiche, substitute one 6-oz. package Wakefield® Alaska Crabmeat for the shrimp. Or, in place of 1 cup half-and-half, use ¾ cup half-and-half and ¼ cup dry sherry.

Swiss and Bacon Squares

Bisquick® suggested this "no time to cook" recipe for a luncheon or supper dish. I put it under Appetizers because it's great cut into bite-size squares and served warm as a "go with" for wine, beer or just about anything else you care to serve.

2 cups Bisquick® Baking	1 lb. bacon, crisply fried
Mix	and crumbled
½ cup cold water	4 eggs
1 8-oz. package natural	½ cup milk
Swiss cheese slices	½ tsp. onion salt

Heat oven to 425°F. Grease baking dish, 13 × 9 × 2 inches. Mix baking mix and water until soft dough forms; beat vigorously 20 strokes. Gently smooth into ball on floured cloth-covered board. Knead 10 times. Pat in dish with floured hands, pressing ½ inch up sides. Top with cheese slices, overlapping edges; sprinkle with bacon; mix remaining ingredients; pour over bacon. Bake until edges are golden brown and knife inserted near center comes out clean, about 20 minutes. Makes 6 to 8 servings as a main course or 12 to 16 servings as an appetizer.

Rumaki Canapés

Americans discovered Rumaki appetizers about 10 years ago, but while great tasting they were troublesome to make. Not so these Ramaki Canapés. The recipe is from those clever Underwood® cooks—easy to prepare and devilishly good.

2 4¾-oz. cans of
   Underwood® Liverwurst Spread
2 tsps. soy sauce
½ tsp. brown sugar
¼ cup chopped water chestnuts
½ lb. raw bacon
   Buttered toast rounds

In a small bowl, combine Liverwurst Spread, soy sauce and brown sugar and mix well. Add water chestnuts and mix. Chill. While mixture is chilling, prepare bacon crumbs. Fry bacon in a frying pan until crisp and let drain on paper toweling. When bacon has cooled, break into small crumbles and set aside. Spoon chilled liverwurst mixture onto prepared toast rounds and top with crumbled bacon. Chill covered until ready to use. Makes 30 hors d'oeuvres.

Deviled Ham Stuffed Cucumbers

The Underwood® Deviled Ham people dreamed up this elegant vegetable appetizer almost 10 years ago, but it's just right for today to serve with drinks.

2 medium cucumbers
1 4½-oz. can Underwood® Deviled Ham
1 hard-cooked egg, coarsely chopped
1 Tbs. finely chopped onion
1 Tbs. finely chopped sour pickle
1 tsp. prepared mustard

Cut cucumbers in half lengthwise and scoop out seeds. In a bowl, mix together deviled ham, chopped egg, onion, pickle and mustard. Spoon mixture into cucumber shells. Chill. When ready to serve, cut cucumber diagonally into 1-inch pieces. Makes about 2 dozen hors d'oeuvres.

Slimster's Guacamole

A long-time favorite from the French® Company. It was especially popular back in the 1940's, and is even more so today when everyone is thinking thin.

1 cup low-fat cottage cheese
1 medium-size avocado, peeled and cut in
　chunks
1 tomato, peeled and cut in chunks
2 Tbs. lemon juice
1 Tbs. French's® Worcestershire Sauce
1 tsp. French's® Garlic Salt
⅛ tsp. French's® Cayenne Pepper
　Cauliflowerets, carrot sticks, celery sticks,
　green or red pepper squares, green onions,
　cucumber sticks.

Combine cottage cheese, avocado, tomato, lemon juice, Worcestershire Sauce, Garlic Salt, and Cayenne Pepper in blender; blend until smooth. Serve as dip with vegetables. Makes about 2 cups dip (about 300 calories per cup).

Almond Cheese Pinecone

The full-page color ad in national magazines showing this absolutely beautiful appetizer sent literally thousands of cooks to the market for Blue Diamond® Almonds. It's terrific—a show-stopper and crowd-pleaser for sure.

2 8-oz. packages cream cheese, softened
2 5-oz. jars pasteurized
  process cheese spread with pimiento
½ lb. blue cheese, crumbled
¼ cup minced green onion
½ tsp. Worcestershire sauce
2 cups Blue Diamond® Blanched Whole
  Almonds, toasted
  Pine sprigs for garnish
  Crackers

In large bowl with mixer at medium speed, beat cream cheese, cheese spread with pimiento and blue cheese until smooth. With spoon, stir in green onions and Worcestershire sauce. Cover and refrigerate about one hour. On work surface, with hands, shape cheese mixture into shape of large pinecone. Arrange on wooden board. Beginning at narrow end of cone, carefully press almonds about ¼ inch deep into cheese mixture in rows, making sure that pointed end of each almond extends at a slight angle. Continue pressing almonds into cheese mixture in rows, with rows slightly overlapping, until all cheese is covered. Garnish pinecone with pine sprigs. Serve with crackers. Makes about 25 servings.

Toasty Bread Slices

This isn't so much a recipe as simply an idea—but what an idea! For anything from a full-scale Italian meal to a TV snack, to go with your favorite beverage: a glass of red wine, an icy cold beer or a chilly mug of milk, from Parkay®.

½ cup soft Parkay® Margarine
⅓ cup crushed French fried onions
 1 Vienna bread loaf, sliced

Combine margarine and onions; spread on one side of each bread slice. Place bread slices spread-side up on ungreased cookie sheet. Bake at 400°F. 12 to 15 minutes or until lightly browned.

Variation: Substitute ⅓ cup Kraft Grated Parmesan Cheese for onions.

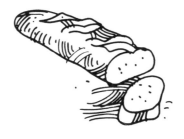

Mushroom Bread

A unique bread from the Kraft® kitchens that resembles a pizza without sauce. Serve as an hors d'oeuvre or cut into small wedges as a snack.

 1 8-oz. can refrigerated crescent rolls
 2 cups mushroom slices
¼ cup margarine, melted
   Kraft® Grated Parmesan Cheese
¼ tsp. marjoram

Separate dough into triangles. Place on ungreased 12-inch pizza pan; press out dough to fit pan. Toss mushrooms with margarine; arrange on dough. Sprinkle with cheese and marjoram. Bake at 375°F. 20 to 25 minutes.

Variations: Shredded Mozzarella, Monterey Jack or Swiss cheese are excellent alternates for Parmesan.

Cocktail Meatballs

So simple and so good. These meatballs from *Campbell's*® *100 Best Recipes* cookbook can be shaped, browned and refrigerated hours before the party. Then it's a breeze to heat them in sauce shortly before serving.

1 lb. ground beef
1 egg, slightly beaten
2 Tbs. fine dry bread
  crumbs
½ tsp. salt
½ cup finely chopped onion
⅓ cup finely chopped green
  pepper

2 Tbs. butter or margarine
1 10¾-oz. can Campbell's®
  Condensed Tomato Soup
2 Tbs. brown sugar
1 Tbs. vinegar
1 Tbs. Worcestershire sauce
1 tsp. prepared mustard
  Dash hot pepper sauce

Mix thoroughly beef, egg, bread crumbs and salt; shape into 50 small ½-inch meatballs. Arrange in shallow baking pan (12 × 8 × 2 inches). Broil 4 inches from heat until browned; turn once. Pour off fat. Meanwhile, in saucepan, cook onion and green pepper in butter until tender. Add meatballs and remaining ingredients. Cover; cook over low heat 10 minutes. Stir occasionally. Makes about 3½ cups.

Pepperoni Pizzas

A fast-food favorite from Hellmann's® and Best Foods® Real Mayonnaise to make at home.

1 cup shredded Mozzarella cheese
   (about 4 ozs.)
1 cup sliced pitted ripe olives
4 ounces pepperoni, chopped
½ cup Hellmann's® Best Foods® Real
   Mayonnaise
¼ tsp. Italian seasoning
4 English muffins, split, toasted

In medium bowl stir together first 5 ingredients. Spoon onto muffin halves. Broil 6 inches from source of heat about 5 minutes or until browned. Makes 8.

Texas Style Pizza

The French® Company combined two favorites of mine—chili and pizza—to come up with this new classic.

½ lb. ground beef
1 envelope French's®
   Chili-O Seasoning Mix
1 16-oz. can tomatoes
1 15-oz. can kidney beans,
   drained and rinsed

1 package active dry yeast
¾ cup warm water
2¼ cups biscuit mix
½ cup corn meal
   Shredded Cheddar or
   American cheese

Brown ground beef in large skillet, stirring to crumble; pour off excess fat. Stir in seasoning mix, tomatoes and beans; simmer, uncovered, 10 minutes. Sprinkle yeast over warm water in large mixing bowl; stir to dissolve. Add biscuit mix and corn meal; stir until smooth. Knead 25 strokes on floured surface. Divide in half, roll or pat each to a 14-inch circle on greased pizza pan or baking sheet. Spoon filling on top of crust; sprinkle with cheese. Bake at 425°F. for 15 to 20 minutes, until crust is golden brown. Makes 6 to 8 servings.

Easy Deep-Dish Pizza

Takes no longer to make than a trip to the local pizzeria and is twice as good. This recipe showed up everywhere—on the box, in national ads and in the *Creative Recipes with Bisquick*® book—and was a smash hit then as it is now.

3 cups Bisquick® Baking
   Mix
¾ cup cold water
1 lb. ground beef
½ cup chopped onion
½ tsp. salt
2 cloves garlic, crushed
1 15-oz. can tomato sauce

1 tsp. Italian seasoning
1 4½-oz. jar sliced
   mushrooms, drained
½ cup chopped green
   pepper
2 cups shredded Mozzarella
   cheese (about 8 ozs.)

Heat oven to 425°F. Lightly grease jelly roll pan, 15½ × 10½ × 1 inch, or cookie sheet. Mix baking mix and water until soft dough forms; beat vigorously 20 strokes. Gently smooth dough into ball on floured cloth-covered board. Knead 20 times. Pat dough in bottom and up sides of pan with floured hands. Or roll into rectangle, 13 × 10 inches, and place on cookie sheet; pinch edges of rectangle, forming ¾-inch rim. Cook and stir ground beef, onion, salt and garlic until beef is brown. Mix tomato sauce and Italian seasoning; spread over dough. Spoon beef mixture over sauce. Top with remaining ingredients. Bake until crust is golden brown, about 20 minutes. Makes 8 servings.

Sour Cream Pizza Strips

A 1979 third-prize winner of Borden's® Contest for recipes using sour cream. These strips taste super good and there's this bonus: they can be made ahead and reheated.

2 cups biscuit baking mix
⅔ cup Borden® Milk
1 tsp. Italian seasoning
1 8-oz. container Borden® Sour Cream
⅓ cup mayonnaise or salad dressing

¼ cup Borden® Grated Parmesan and Romano Cheese
¼ cup chopped onion
3 Tbs. chopped pimiento
1 Tbs. chopped parsley
½ tsp. garlic powder

Preheat oven to 400°F. In medium bowl, combine baking mix, Milk and Italian seasoning; stir to make soft dough. Turn onto well-floured surface; knead lightly 10 to 12 strokes. Pat dough onto bottom and up sides of greased 13 × 9-inch baking dish, making a small rim. In medium bowl, mix remaining ingredients; spread evenly over dough. Bake 20 to 25 minutes or until golden. Cut into rectangles. Serve warm. Refrigerate leftovers.

Chili Quesadilla

Quesadilla is Mexico's answer to Italian Pizza and French Quiche. This is Hormel's® adaptation. Best served hot, good any way.

2 10 to 12-inch prepared flour tortillas
1 15-oz. can Hormel® Chili (with beans or no beans)
1 Tbs. chopped onion
½ tsp. garlic powder
2 tsp. green chilies, chopped

½ cup Monterey Jack cheese, grated
½ cup Cheddar cheese, grated
Red onion rings

Bake tortillas in 350°F. oven 2 minutes per side. Heat Hormel® Chili, adding onion, garlic powder, chilies. Sprinkle Monterey Jack cheese over tortillas, then spread thinly on chili mixture. Sprinkle Cheddar cheese on top, heat 8 minutes in 350°F. oven. Garnish with red onion rings.

A PAIR OF PLANTERS® TEX-MEX FAST-FOOD SPECIALS

For the past five years requests have been pouring in to the Planters® test kitchens for easy to prepare "Tex-Mex" recipes. Here are two of their most popular. They are super delicious as well as fast and easy to make.

Beef Tacos

2 Tbs. Planters® Peanut Oil	1 tsp. salt
1 lb. ground beef	Generous dash ground black pepper
½ cup chopped onion	12 prepared taco shells
1 medium clove garlic, minced	Grated cheese
1 8-oz. can tomato sauce	Shredded lettuce

Heat Planters® Peanut Oil in skillet over medium-high heat. Add ground beef and brown, stirring to break up beef. Add onion and garlic; continue cooking until onion is tender. Mix in tomato sauce, salt and pepper. Heat, stirring occasionally. Spoon beef mixture into prepared taco shells. Top with cheese and lettuce. Serve hot. Makes 12 servings.

Chicken Enchiladas

⅓ cup Planters® Peanut Oil
½ cup finely chopped onion
2 cloves garlic, crushed
½ cup flour
1 13¼-oz. can chicken broth
1⅔ cups water
½ cup enchilada sauce
1 Tbs. chili powder
½ tsp. salt
1¼ cups coarsely shredded Cheddar cheese (about 5 ozs.)
1½ cups diced cooked chicken or turkey
¼ cup sliced pitted ripe olives
8 7-inch Piñata® Corn Tortillas

Heat Planters® Peanut Oil in a saucepan over medium heat; add onion and garlic and cook until tender. Stir in flour, mixing until smooth. Gradually add chicken broth, water and enchilada sauce, mixing until smooth. Stir in chili powder and salt. Cook over medium heat, stirring constantly, until thick. Reserving ½ cup cheese, mix remaining cheese with chicken and olives. Dip Piñata® Corn Tortillas in prepared sauce for about 5 seconds. Spoon 3 Tbs. chicken filling across center of each; roll up and place seam side down, in a shallow 2½-quart baking dish. Pour remaining sauce over tortillas. Bake at 350°F. for 15 minutes. Sprinkle with reserved cheese and continue baking 10 minutes. Garnish with sliced ripe olives if desired and serve immediately. Makes 4 servings.

A.1.® INTERNATIONAL STEAKBURGERS

- -

From the A.1.® Steak Sauce people comes this original Californian idea for "super plus" hamburgers. I've also included three variations—all equally good.

Basic A.1.® Hamburgers

1½ lbs. ground beef
1½ tsps. salt (optional)
¼ cup A.1.® Steak Sauce

In medium bowl, lightly combine all ingredients. Form 6 patties to fit bread shape of your choice. Broil, barbecue or pan fry until cooked as desired. Makes 6.

English Cheddar Burgers

1 cup shredded sharp yellow Cheddar cheese
  (4 ozs.)
2 Tbs. minced fresh onion
1 medium clove garlic, crushed
2 Tbs. A.1.® Steak Sauce
6 Basic A.1.® Hamburgers, cooked
6 English muffins, fork split, toasted and
  buttered

Combine cheese, onion, garlic and A.1. Spread 2 Tbs. over each cooked hamburger patty. Broil to melt cheese. Serve on muffins. Makes 6.

Greek Burgers

1 cup (4 ozs.) Feta cheese, rinsed and crumbled
¼ cup sliced ripe olives
1 Tbs. A.1.® Steak Sauce
1 tsp. lemon juice
2 Tbs. mayonnaise

6 Basic A.1.® Hamburgers, cooked
3 Pita (or pocket) bread, cut in half
6 tomato slices
   Shredded lettuce

Combine cheese, olives, A.1.®, lemon juice and mayonnaise. Place hamburgers in Pita bread. Spoon topping over hamburgers. Heat in preheated 425°F. oven 5 minutes. Garnish with tomato and lettuce. Makes 6.

Lipton® Onion Burgers

A famous Lipton® Onion Soup mix combination that has become an American classic.

1 envelope Lipton® Onion Soup mix
½ cup water
2 lbs. ground beef

In large bowl, combine Onion Soup mix, water and ground beef. Shape into 8 patties. Grill or broil until done. Makes 8 servings.

San Francisco Burgers

2 large, ripe avocados, peeled and mashed
2 Tbs. A.1.® Steak Sauce
½ tsp. salt
¼ cup minced fresh onion
4 slices bacon, cooked, drained, and crumbled

6 Basic A.1.® Hamburgers, cooked
6 tomato slices
12 slices San Francisco sour-dough bread, toasted

Combine avocado, A.1.®, salt, onion, and bacon. Serve hamburgers, topped with sauce and tomato, on toast. Makes 6.

Corned Beef Funburger

What's a funburger? It's a hamburger with a super great-tasting filling. It's an Underwood® theory that makes sense and great eating.

3 hamburger rolls, sliced, heated
1 4½-oz. can Underwood® Corned Beef Spread
¾ tsp. horseradish
3 Tbs. chopped walnuts
3 green pepper rings
3 Tbs. drained crushed pineapple

Partially hollow top half of each roll. Combine corned beef spread and horseradish, spread on bottom half. Sprinkle corned beef mixture with nuts, top with a pepper ring, fill ring with pineapple and cover with top half of roll. Makes 3 sandwiches.

Hamburgers Angostura

Dione Lucas made her original recipe for Hamburger Angostura® famous on TV in the late 1950's.

2 lbs. ground beef
2 tsps. salt
½ tsp. pepper
2 tsps. Angostura®
½ cup ice water

Combine meat with salt and pepper. Mix Angostura® with ice water and pour over meat. Blend thoroughly and shape into 8 patties. Broil or pan-fry hamburgers quickly to desired degree of doneness. Serve hot with sauce (below):

Sauce

1 8-oz. can tomato sauce
¼ cup water
1 tsp. Angostura®
1 Tbs. minced onion
2 Tbs. minced green pepper
2 Tbs. minced celery

Combine all ingredients and simmer 10 minutes. Makes 8 patties.

Super Burger Topper

Every time I've ever served this burger topping someone wants the recipe, and that someone usually gives it to someone else. The good cook at Heinz® who dreamed it up should be given a medal by hamburger fans.

½ cup chopped green
  pepper
¼ cup chopped onion
1 Tbs. salad oil
½ cup Heinz® Tomato
  Ketchup

⅓ cup water
½ tsp. chili powder
¼ tsp. salt

Sauté green pepper and onion in salad oil until tender. Stir in ketchup, water, chili powder and salt; simmer 10 to 15 minutes, stirring occasionally. Serve on hot dogs, hamburgers or other meat sandwiches. Makes about 1 cup.

Bavarian Wranglers® Franks

Here's a new one to me, but it may not be to you. It was printed on the Wranglers® package a few years ago.

4 Wranglers® Smoked Franks
1⅓ cups prepared German potato salad
2 Tbs. chopped parsley
4 slices crusty French bread
   Hormel bacon bits

Split meaty, smoky-tasting Wranglers® Franks almost to one end. Slash sides lightly and form into circle, fastening with toothpicks. Place on baking sheet. Stir parsley into potato salad; spoon ⅓ cup into each frank. Bake 10 minutes at 350°F. Top each bread slice with stuffed frank; garnish with bacon bits. Makes 4.

Spicy Muffins

A nosh, a snack, a sandwich—you name it. It's a new classic from a new company, Frieda's of California, and you most certainly will want the recipe in your permanent file of great quick and easy recipes.

1½ cups cottage cheese
½ cup wheat germ
2 Tbs. chopped chilies
¼ tsp. basil, dried and crushed
¼ tsp. oregano
¼ tsp. salt
4 to 6 whole wheat English muffin halves,
   toasted
   tomato slices
   Cheddar cheese slices
   Minced parsley

Combine first 6 ingredients and mound on English muffin halves. On each muffin, place a slice of tomato and criss-cross with 2 strips of sliced Cheddar cheese. Broil 3 to 4 inches from source of heat for 5 minutes, or until cheese melts. Sprinkle with minced parsley. Makes 4 to 6 open-faced sandwiches.

Vegetable Rarebit

A 1940's classic, from the second edition of the *Pet*® *Evaporated Milk Cookbook*. Quick, easy and so good—a hearty snack supper dish to please just about everyone.

	For 2	For 4	For 6
Grated American cheese or sliced, packaged variety	1 cup (3 ozs.)	1¾ cups (5 ozs.)	2½ cups (½ lb.)
Pet® Milk	¼ cup	½ cup	¾ cup
Salt	¼ tsp.	½ tsp.	¾ tsp.
Dry mustard	¼ tsp.	½ tsp.	¾ tsp.
Kidney beans, drained and canned*	¾ cup	1½ cups	2¼ cups
Bread, white or whole wheat	2 slices	4 slices	6 slices
Fresh tomatoes, cut in ½-inch slices**	1 large	2 large	3 large
Salt	⅛ tsp.	¼ tsp.	½ tsp.
Pepper	few grains	few grains	⅛ tsp.

* Cooked, dried red, pink or kidney beans may also be used. You will need to soak about 6 hours or overnight ⅓ cup beans in 1¾ cups water for 2, ⅔ cup beans in 3 cups water for 4 and 1 cup beans in 4 cups water for 6. In the morning, add ¼ tsp. salt for 2, ½ tsp. salt for 4, and ¾ tsp. salt for 6, then cover and boil 1 hour or until tender.

** Drained canned tomatoes may be used in place of fresh tomatoes. You will need ⅔ cup for 2, 1⅓ cups for 4 and 2 cups for 6.

For cheese sauce, mix together grated cheese, Pet® Milk, salt and dry mustard. Cook over boiling water until cheese melts and mixture is smooth, stirring frequently. Add kidney beans and keep warm until needed. Turn on oven and set at 375°F. Toast bread on one side only, then put bread, toasted side up, in shallow baking pan. Arrange sliced tomatoes on top of toast and sprinkle with salt and pepper. Bake until tomatoes are thoroughly heated, about 5 minutes. Put on serving plates and serve at once with cheese sauce.

French's® Tomato Rarebit

My mother always served rarebits after a night of dancing to a big-name band at the local country club. Great these days while watching the late show on TV.

2 large tomatoes, halved
  Sugar
  Salt and freshly ground
  pepper
2 Tbs. (¼ stick) butter
1 Tbs. prepared mustard
½ tsp. dry mustard
2 tsps. French's®
  Worcestershire Sauce
½ tsp. paprika

¼ tsp. salt
1 lb. sharp Cheddar
  cheese, cut into ½-inch
  cubes
½ cup beer or ale
2 egg yolks
¼ cup whipping cream or
  milk
  Toast

Preheat broiler. Sprinkle tomatoes generously with sugar, salt and pepper. Place on baking sheet and broil just until tender, turning once to cook both sides. Turn oven to low and keep tomatoes warm. Melt butter in top of double boiler or chafing dish over simmering water. Add mustards, Worcestershire, paprika and salt and stir well to blend. Add cheese, making sure water does not boil or cheese will become tough. (Some stringiness may occur, but mixture will incorporate as cheese warms.) Allow most of cheese to melt, stirring frequently. Add beer and continue stirring until cheese is completely melted. Beat yolks with cream and add slowly to cheese mixture, stirring until blended and thickened. Spoon immediately over warm tomatoes. Arrange toast around edge of dish. Makes 4 servings.

Chicken and Asparagus Rarebit

Very elegant and great-tasting too. A party dish that can come from your emergency shelf whenever there are unexpected guests. The idea is from Swanson® and it's such a good one it's proven to be one of their most popular recipes.

1 10¾-oz. can Campbell's® Condensed Cream
   of Chicken Soup
¼ cup water
1 cup shredded Cheddar cheese
1 5-oz can Swanson® Chunk Chicken
   Cooked asparagus spears
   Toast

In saucepan, combine soup, water and cheese. Heat until cheese melts; stir occasionally. Add chicken; heat. Arrange asparagus on toast; pour chicken mixture over asparagus. Makes about 2½ cups, or 3 servings.

Cheese Fondue

The nice thing about this lovely fondue is that it won't get stringy, separate or become gummy as ordinary fondues are apt to do. From *Campbell's*® *100 Best Recipes* cookbook.

1 cup Sauterne or other dry white wine
1 large clove garlic, minced
1 lb. natural Swiss cheese, cubed or shredded
¼ cup flour
1 11-oz. can Campbell's® Condensed Cheddar
  Cheese Soup
  French or Italian bread cubes*

In saucepan or fondue pot, simmer wine and garlic. Combine cheese and flour; gradually blend into wine. Heat until cheese melts; stir often. Blend in soup. Heat, stirring until smooth. Spear bread with fork or toothpick and dip into fondue. Makes about 4 cups.

* Also use bite-size pieces of cooked artichoke hearts, franks, lobster or shrimp.

Unsalted Nut Butter

People write Planters® Peanut test kitchens every day for the "how-to" of nut butters. This one is elegant, tastes divine and is good for you, too—no salt is added.

2 cups Planters® Dry Roasted Unsalted Cashews
  or Unsalted Peanuts
3 Tbs. Planters® Oil
1 tsp. honey

Place Planters® Dry Roasted Unsalted Cashews or Unsalted Peanuts in blender or food processor. Blend on high speed until coarsely chopped. Continue blending, adding Planters® Oil in a steady stream. Add honey and blend until smooth and creamy. Makes ¼ cup.

2.
The Main Dish: Meats, Poultry, Fish and Seafood, Sauces and Meatless Main Courses

There are still a few people in this country who persist in putting food, especially main course dishes, into separate categories such as "gourmet" food, "health" food, "convenience" food and such. They even go as far as to separate family food from party food; but this is ridiculous. Except for personal preference and/or prejudice there are only two kinds of food: truly flavorful and satisfying food and food that is disappointingly dull. Truly flavorful food *is* gourmet food and only healthful food is really satisfying. Whether it is convenient and thrifty besides depends very much on the recipe used, but with know-how it can be not one but all of these things.

Each recipe in this chapter was developed by an expert and very knowledgeable cook who "knew how" to make it a multi-category dish: flavorful, healthful, easy to prepare, relatively economical even in these inflated times and, especially, convenient for you, the cook. In fact these are no ordinary recipes; from a simple, but simply superb, Irish Stew developed by James Beard, no less, to a very continental Steak with Fresh Tomato Sauce from the Pompeian® Olive Oil Company, they are very special indeed. Each one is a more-for-your-money dish, satisfying, kind to your pocketbook and easily prepared.

We lead off with beef and some really splendid ways to put the ultimate main course on your table; recipes for flavorful, juicy, tender and affordable steaks—all old favorites from labels or advertisements. Following these an elegant Beef En Brochette, perfect for guests or a "special" dinner; then some thrifty, old-fashioned, richly flavored recipes for stews, short ribs and such; plus recipes which will transform ground beef into the most requested dishes in your home.

But that's only the beginning; there are also over twenty "asked for" recipes for veal, lamb, pork and ham and over twenty more easy, expert and extra special ones for poultry, fish and seafood, and meatless main courses, too. You'll enjoy cooking and serving, each one and every one you serve will be truly enjoyed and be asked for a repeat performance.

Marinated Steak

A truly inspired way to transform a tough chuck steak into as tender and flavorful a steak as any you've ever eaten. The recipe is on the label of Regina® Cooking Sherry—has been for years.

1 1½-lb. flank, London broil or chuck steak
½ cup *each* Regina® Cooking Sherry and
     Japanese Soy Sauce
2 Tbs. cooking oil
1 large clove garlic, minced
¼ tsp. ground ginger

Score steak in criss-cross pattern on both sides. Combine remaining ingredients in shallow dish. Marinate steak, covered, for several hours or overnight. Turn occasionally. Grill or broil until cooked as desired. Serves 6.

Beefsteak with Fresh Tomato Sauce

Here's a Continental way with steak from Pompeian® Olive Oil, and a tip for cutting the cost of a steak dinner; substitute inexpensive, thin-sliced bottom round steak for more expensive cuts and serve both steak and sauce over rice. Elegant and delicious.

2 lbs. ripe tomatoes, peeled
     and chopped coarsely
2 Tbs. Pompeian® Olive Oil
4 garlic cloves, sliced
     Salt

Pepper
Oregano
Fresh basil or parsley to
taste
6 small rump or sirloin steaks

Cook tomatoes, Pompeian® Olive Oil, garlic, salt and pepper until tomatoes are soft and begin to give off their juice. Add oregano, fresh basil or parsley to taste, if desired. Pound small rump or sirloin steaks until they are about ¼-inch thick, season with salt and pepper, and pan broil quickly in small amount of Pompeian® Olive Oil to the desired stage of doneness. Spread the tomato sauce over steaks, cover the pan and cook the steaks for about 5 minutes, or longer if a tougher cut of beef is used. Serve very hot with the sauce. Serves 6.

Flank Steak Creole

A great way to make inexpensive flank steak into a superb tasting and positively elegant entrée. Pepperidge Farm® put it on their Herb Seasoned Stuffing Mix over a dozen years ago.

1½ to 2½ lbs. flank steak
⅓ cup butter or margarine
2 Tbs. chopped onion
2 Tbs. chopped green pepper
1 Tbs. tomato paste
½ tsp. horseradish
½ tsp. salt
¼ tsp. sugar

½ cup water
2 cups Pepperidge Farm® Herb Seasoned Stuffing Mix
1 10½-oz. can condensed beef broth
1 Tbs. tomato paste
1½ Tbs. corn starch

Preheat oven to 500°F. Score one side of steak in a diamond pattern and rub with salt and pepper. Melt butter in a saucepan and sauté onion and green pepper until tender. Stir in 1 Tbs. tomato paste, horseradish, salt, sugar, water and stuffing. Place mixture down center on unscored side of steak, but not quite to the ends. Fold ends over stuffing, then bring together and overlap long sides. Skewer together. Place in a shallow baking pan and roast for 15 minutes. Reduce heat to 350°F. and continue baking 40 to 50 minutes. Meanwhile, combine beef broth, remaining tomato paste and corn starch in a saucepan. Bring to a boil, stirring, and boil 1 minute until shiny and thickened. Pass with the sliced steak. Makes 4 to 6 servings.

Easy-Does-it Swiss Steak

An all-time Hunt-Wesson® favorite and not just because it's simple to prepare, but because it tastes simply superb.

3 Tbs. pure vegetable oil
2 lbs. round steak, 1-inch thick
¼ cup flour
1 envelope dry onion soup mix
1 8-oz. can Hunt's® Tomato Sauce
½ cup water

Pour oil in 7½ × 12 × 1½-inch baking dish. Place in oven at 400°F. While dish and oil heat, trim steak and pound 2 Tbs. flour into each side. Place in heated baking dish; turn to coat both sides. Sprinkle on soup mix. Pour Hunt's® Tomato Sauce mixed with water over all. Cover tightly. Reduce oven temperature to 325°F. Bake 2½ to 3 hours until fork tender. Skim excess fat from gravy. Makes 6 servings.

Beef en Brochette

One of the most popular recipes to ever appear on the Heinz® 57 Sauce bottle. Serve over rice, add a glass of red wine to the menu, and your guests and family will be impressed by the simple elegance of this delicious meal.

1 13¼-oz. can pineapple
chunks
½ cup Heinz® 57 Sauce
2 Tbs. dry white wine
1 Tbs. salad oil
½ tsp. salt

Dash pepper
2 lbs. beef sirloin tip or top
round, cut into 1-inch
cubes
Salt and pepper

Drain pineapple, reserving ½ cup liquid. Cover and refrigerate pineapple chunks. Combine the ½ cup pineapple liquid with Heinz® 57 Sauce and next 4 ingredients; pour over meat. Marinate 2 to 3 hours in refrigerator, turning occasionally. Thread meat and pineapple chunks alternately on six (12-inch) skewers, allowing 4 to 5 pieces of meat and 5 to 6 pieces of pineapple for each skewer. Brush with marinade; season lightly with salt and pepper. Grill or broil 3 inches from heat source 5 minutes on each side for medium rare. Makes 6 servings.

Grits and Grillades

This is South Louisiana cooking at its very best. The recipe was developed by people who truly know fine food—The McIlhenny's, who make Tabasco® Hot Pepper Sauce in Louisiana's Cajun country.

2 lbs. beef round, thinly
sliced
6 Tbs. bacon drippings or
salad oil
4 Tbs. all-purpose flour
1 medium onion, chopped
1 cup peeled and cubed
tomatoes
1½ cups water

1 green pepper, chopped
1 clove garlic, chopped
1 bay leaf
1 Tbs. chopped parsley
2 tsps. salt
1 tsp. Tabasco® Hot Pepper
Sauce
½ tsp. thyme
3 cups hot cooked grits

Brown meat in oil in deep skillet. Remove meat. Add flour and brown, stirring constantly. Add onion and tomatoes. Simmer a few minutes. Add meat, water, pepper, garlic, bay leaf, parsley, salt, Tabasco® Hot Pepper Sauce and thyme. Cover and simmer for 1½ hours or until meat is very tender, adding water if necessary to make sauce the consistency of thick gravy. Serve grillades with portion of hot grits on the side. Serves 4 to 6.

Note: If you live in a part of the country where grits are not available, you may serve grillades with hot cooked rice.

Hungarian Goulash

This easy to prepare goulash has been a favorite for years in the Pet® Milk Company Consumer Services Kitchen. It's hard to believe, but the original version appeared in their *Pet® Gold Cookbook* back in 1932.

1½ lbs. round steak, cut in
　　½-inch cubes
3 Tbs. oil
⅓ cup all-purpose flour
1 Tbs. paprika
1 tsp. salt
¼ tsp. pepper

¼ tsp. garlic powder
1 medium onion, thinly
　　sliced
1 1-lb. can whole tomatoes
⅓ cup water
⅔ cup Pet® Evaporated
　　Milk

Brown meat in hot oil in large saucepan. Mix together flour, paprika, salt, pepper and garlic powder. Stir into meat mixture. Add onion, tomatoes and water. Cover. Simmer 1 hour, stirring occasionally. Gradually stir Pet®

Evaporated Milk into hot mixture. Simmer 15 minutes, stirring frequently. Serve over hot buttered noodles. Makes 6½-cup servings.

Hungarian Pot Roast

This super-flavored pot roast recipe has been on the top twenty "most wanted" lists at the Hunt-Wesson® test kitchens for over 15 years.

1 3- to 4-lb. lean chuck or rump roast	8 small carrots, pared
1½ tsp. paprika	2 8-oz cans Hunt's® Tomato Sauce with Mushrooms
2 tsps. salt	1 clove garlic, minced
¼ tsp. pepper	½ tsp. onion salt
2 Tbs. pure vegetable oil	2 Tbs. minced parsley
½ cup water	1 cup sour cream (optional)
1 bay leaf	
8 to 10 small whole white onions	

Trim excess fat from meat. Sprinkle with paprika, salt and pepper. Brown in oil in Dutch oven over medium heat. Add water and bay leaf; simmer, covered, 2 hours or until meat is almost tender. Skim off fat. Place onions and carrots around meat. Add Hunt's® Sauce, garlic and onion salt. Cover; simmer 50 to 60 minutes longer until meat and vegetables are tender. Add parsley. Just before serving, remove from heat and gradually stir in sour cream, if desired. Makes 6 to 8 servings.

Roast Chuck Neapolitan

**One of the easiest recipes ever to appear on a Campbell's®
Soup label and one of the best tasting ways you'll ever find to
cook this inexpensive cut of meat.**

1 3½-lb. boned chuck roast
(about 2 inches thick)
2 Tbs. shortening
1 10¾-oz. can Campbell's®
Condensed Tomato Soup

½ cup water
1 cup sliced onion
1 large clove garlic, minced
2 tsps. oregano, crushed
Generous dash pepper

In large heavy pan, brown meat in shortening. Pour off
fat. Stir in remaining ingredients. Cover; cook over low
heat 2½ hours or until tender. Spoon off fat. Thicken
sauce if desired. Makes 6 servings.

Oven-Baked Short Ribs
with Garden Vegetables

**I always thought this was my mother's "own" original
recipe—until it was sent to me by an old friend who had long
ago clipped it from the Argo-Kingsford® Corn Starch box.**

3 lbs. beef short ribs
1 tsp. salt
¼ tsp. pepper
1 lb. carrots, cleaned and
halved
1 lb. potatoes, pared and
halved
½ lb. fresh green beans

4 small white onions
1 13¾-oz. can beef broth
2 tsps. prepared mustard
2 Tbs. horseradish
2 Tbs. Argo-Kingsford's®
Corn Starch
¼ cup water

Trim excess fat from meat. Place in 13 × 9 × 2-inch baking pan; sprinkle with salt and pepper. Bake uncovered
in 350°F. oven 2 hours; drain fat. Add next 4 ingredients.
Mix broth, horseradish and mustard; pour over meat and

vegetables. Cover with foil; bake 1 to 1½ hours longer or until tender. Arrange meat and vegetables on serving platter; keep warm. Strain broth; remove excess fat. Add water, if necessary, to make 2 cups and return to baking pan. Mix Corn Starch and ¼ cup cool water; stir into pan. Bring to boil 1 minute. Serve gravy with meat and vegetables. Makes 4 servings.

Po-Man's Ribs and Rice

A very popular "stick to the ribs" kind of recipe. Up-dated by home-economists at the Tabasco® Test Kitchens.

2 to 3 lbs. short ribs
1 10½-oz. can condensed
  onion soup
1 4-oz. can mushrooms
1 cup beef bouillon

½ tsp. salt
½ to 1 tsp. Tabasco® Hot
  Pepper Sauce
Hot cooked rice

Brown short ribs in Dutch oven. Combine remaining ingredients except rice, plus ½ cup water. Pour over ribs. Cover and simmer about 2½ hours. Serve with hot cooked rice. Makes 4 servings.

Salisbury Steak, Onion Gravy

Remember Salisbury steak? This label recipe comes from *Campbell's® 100 Best Recipes* cookbook.

1 10½-oz. can
  Campbell's® Condensed
  Onion Soup
1½ lbs. ground beef
½ cup fine dry bread
  crumbs
1 egg, slightly beaten
¼ tsp. salt

Dash pepper
1 Tbs. flour
¼ cup catsup
¼ cup water
1 tsp. Worcestershire
  sauce
½ tsp. prepared mustard

In bowl, combine ⅓ cup Soup with beef, crumbs, egg, salt and pepper. Shape into 6 oval patties. In skillet, brown patties; pour off fat. Gradually blend remaining soup into flour until smooth. Add to skillet with remaining ingredients; stir to loosen browned bits. Cover; cook over low heat 20 minutes or until done. Stir occasionally. Makes 6 servings.

Skillet Stuffed Peppers

From one of the most popular booklets ever printed by the A.1.® Sauce people. It's recipes like this that make for easy preparation and grand eating.

½ cup converted rice, cooked
¾ lb. ground beef
¼ cup minced, fresh onion
3 Tbs. A.1.® Steak Sauce
1 tsp. salt
¼ tsp. pepper
1 8-oz. can tomato sauce

1 12-oz. can whole kernel corn, drained
6 large green peppers
6 medium carrots, peeled and cut into 1-inch pieces
3 Tbs. butter (or margarine)
½ cup water

While rice is cooking, in medium skillet brown beef until crumbly. Drain. Add onion. Cook until onion is soft. Remove from heat. Mix in A.1.®, salt, pepper, tomato sauce, corn and rice. Cut tops, seeds and membranes from peppers. Discard. Fill peppers with meat and rice mixture. In 10-inch skillet, place peppers and carrots. Add butter and water. Simmer, covered, 30 to 40 minutes, or until carrots are tender. Serves 6.

Saucy Meatballs

Adapt this recipe to your next party by serving it from a chafing dish with cocktail picks and omitting the noodles. It's from Heinz® 57 Sauce and has been a 4-star favorite for over ten years.

1 lb. lean ground beef
⅔ cup grated Parmesan
  cheese
½ cup seasoned dry bread
  crumbs
½ cup milk
1 egg, slightly beaten
2 Tbs. shortening

1 Tbs. flour
1 28-ozs. can tomatoes, cut
  into bite-size pieces
⅓ to ½ cup Heinz® 57 Sauce
1 Tbs. sugar
½ tsp. salt
  Hot buttered noodles

Combine first 5 ingredients. Shape into 20 meatballs using a rounded Tbs. for each. Brown well in shortening. Drain excess fat. Sprinkle flour over meatballs; stir gently to coat meatballs. Combine tomatoes, Heinz® 57 Sauce, sugar and salt; pour over meatballs. Simmer uncovered, 25 minutes or until sauce is desired consistency, stirring occasionally. Serve meatballs and sauce over noodles. Makes 5 servings (about 3 cups sauce).

Sweet-Sour Meatballs

Another easy, delicious and different way with meatballs from Heinz®.

1 lb. lean ground beef
1 egg, slightly beaten
1 tsp. salt
  Dash pepper
2 Tbs. shortening
1 medium green pepper,
  cut into strips

1 medium onion, sliced
1½ cups pineapple juice
¼ cup Heinz® 57 Sauce
  Hot buttered rice

Lightly combine first 4 ingredients; form into 16 meatballs. Partially brown meatballs in shortening. Add green pepper and onion; sauté until vegetables are tender. Stir in pineapple juice and Heinz® 57 Sauce. Cover; simmer 15 to 20 minutes or until meatballs are cooked. Thicken sauce with corn starch/water mixture, if desired. Serve over rice. Makes 4 servings.

Cheeseburger Pie

Remember this? It was a teen-age favorite way back before pizza became popular—and it still is. A feature recipe found on the Bisquick® Baking Mix box back in the 1960's.

1 cup Bisquick® Baking Mix
¼ cup cold water
1 lb. ground beef
½ cup chopped onion
½ tsp. salt
¼ tsp. pepper
2 Tbs. Bisquick® Baking Mix

1 Tbs. Worcestershire sauce
2 eggs
1 cup small curd creamed
  cottage cheese
2 medium tomatoes, sliced
1 cup shredded Cheddar
  cheese (about 4 ozs.)

Heat oven to 375°F. Mix 1 cup Bisquick® Baking Mix and the water until soft dough forms; beat vigorously 20 strokes. Gently smooth dough into ball on floured cloth-covered board. Knead 5 times. Roll dough 2 inches larger than inverted pie plate, 9 × 1¼ inches. Ease into plate; flute edge if desired. Cook and stir ground beef and onion until beef is brown; drain. Stir in salt, pepper, 2 Tbs. Bisquick® Baking Mix and the Worcestershire sauce. Spoon into pie crust. Mix eggs and cottage cheese; pour over beef mixture. Arrange tomato slices in circle on top; sprinkle with Cheddar cheese. Bake until set, about 30 minutes. Makes 6 to 8 servings.

Tangy Meat Loaf

A "best of the best" recipes from the Wheat Chex® cereal permanent file of all-time favorites.

½ cup catsup
2 Tbs. brown sugar
½ tsp. powdered mustard
4 tsps. Worcestershire
  sauce
2 tsps. seasoned salt
1½ tsps. onion powder
¼ tsp. garlic powder

¼ tsp. ground black pepper
1 egg
2 Tbs. finely chopped
  green pepper
1½ cups Wheat Chex®
  cereal
1½ lbs. ground beef

In large bowl combine catsup, brown sugar and mustard. Reserve 4 Tbs. mixture for topping. To remaining mixture add Worcestershire sauce, salt, onion, garlic powder, pepper and egg. Blend well. Stir in green pepper and Wheat Chex.® Let stand 5 minutes. Break up Wheat Chex.® Add ground beef. Mix well. Shape into loaf in shallow baking pan. Bake in 350°F. oven for 65 minutes. Spread top with reserved catsup mixture. Bake additional 15 minutes. Makes about 6 servings.

Skillet Barbecued Pork Chops

Simply terrific! One of the first recipes to appear on the Kikkoman® Teriyaki Sauce label. Still one of the best.

6 pork chops, ½-inch thick
1 Tbs. salad oil
¾ cup water
¼ cup Kikkoman® Teriyaki
  Sauce
¼ cup tomato catsup
4 tsps. brown sugar, packed
4 tsps. corn starch

Brown chops slowly in hot oil on both sides; drain. Combine ½ cup water with next 3 ingredients; pour over chops. Cover and simmer 30 minutes; turn chops over and cook 30 minutes longer. Remove from pan. Dissolve corn starch in remaining water; stir into pan. Cook and stir until sauce boils and thickens. Return chops and coat both sides with sauce. Makes 6 servings.

7-Layer Casserole

A recipe for liberated cooks, so quick and easy, developed long before cooks were liberated. So delicious it is one of the most popular ever from the Hunt-Wesson® kitchens.

1 cup uncooked rice
1 1-lb. can whole kernel corn, undrained
1 tsp. seasoned salt
¼ tsp. seasoned pepper
1 beef bouillon cube
¾ cup boiling water
1 15-oz. can Hunt's® Tomato Sauce with Tomato Bits

1 tsp. Worcestershire sauce
1 tsp. Italian herb seasoning
1 cup chopped onion
½ cup each: chopped green pepper and celery
1 lb. lean ground beef
1 cup shredded mild Cheddar cheese
2 Tbs. imitation bacon bits

In 2-quart casserole, arrange ingredients in layers in the following order:

Rice mixed well with corn, half the salt and pepper, bouillon cube and boiling water.

Half of Hunt's® Tomato Sauce that has been mixed with Worcestershire sauce and Italian seasoning.

Chopped onion, green pepper and celery.

Uncooked ground beef, remaining salt and pepper.

Remaining Hunt's® Tomato Sauce mixture. Cover tightly; bake at 375°F. 45 minutes.

Sprinkle with cheese; bake, uncovered, 15 minutes longer.

Top with bacon bits before serving.

Makes 4 to 6 servings.

Silverado Taco Casserole

Would a Texas woman like me pass up this recipe? I found it on a package of Ortega® Taco Shells but, as they told me at the Ortega® test kitchens, so did a couple of 100,000 other aficionados of Tex-Mex food. If you like that South-of-the-Border flavor, you'll love this casserole.

10 Ortega® Taco Shells,
  coarsely broken
1½ lbs. ground beef
 1 1¼-oz. package Ortega®
  Taco Seasoning Mix
 ½ cup water
 2 Tbs. dried minced onion
 1 8-oz. can tomato sauce

2 cups (½ lb.) grated
  Monterey Jack cheese
1 large tomato, cut in
  wedges
6 stuffed green olives,
  sliced
  Ortega® Taco Sauce

In lightly greased 1½-quart casserole, place one half taco chips. Set aside. In 10-inch skillet, brown beef until crumbled. Drain. Add taco seasoning mix and water. Simmer, uncovered, 10 minutes. Stir in onion and tomato sauce. Spoon meat mixture over taco shells. Sprinkle with 1½ cups cheese. Place remaining taco chips over cheese. Sprinkle with remaining cheese. Arrange tomato wedges and olives attractively on top. Bake in preheated 350°F. oven 15 to 20 minutes or until hot and bubbly. Serve with Ortega® Taco Sauce. Makes 6 servings.

Stuffed Cabbage with Creamy Horseradish Sauce

It's positively amazing and really rather wonderful what a good cook can create with no-nonsense supermarket ingredients. This recipe from the A.1.® Sauce test kitchen is a classic example. It's extraordinarily good and positively elegant to look at and serve.

1 firm medium head
   cabbage
1 egg, beaten
1 lb. lean ground beef
3 Tbs. A.1.® Steak Sauce
2 Tbs. horseradish

2 Tbs. minced fresh onion
1 tsp. salt
½ tsp. pepper
2 Tbs. dry bread crumbs
   Creamy Horseradish
   Sauce (below)

Remove damaged outer leaves of cabbage. Slice off 1 inch of cabbage top. Remove inner leaves. Reserve top. Scoop out center of cabbage leaving ¾-inch cabbage shell. Finely chop 1 cup of removed cabbage leaves. Combine remaining ingredients and chopped cabbage. Pack into cabbage cavity. Replace top. Tie stuffed cabbage in cheesecloth. Place on rack, or nest of crinkled foil, in 4-quart saucepan. Pour 2 cups water in bottom of pan. Steam for 1 hour. Remove cheesecloth carefully from cabbage. Cut in wedges and serve with Creamy Horseradish Sauce. Serves 6.

Creamy Horseradish Sauce

¼ cup butter (or margarine)
¼ cup flour
1 tsp. salt
¼ tsp. pepper
2¼ cups milk
2 Tbs. horseradish
1 Tbs. A.1.® Steak Sauce

In 2-quart saucepan, melt butter. Stir in flour. Cook, stirring constantly, for 2 minutes. Add salt, pepper, milk, horseradish and A.1.® Cook, stirring occasionally, until thickened. Spoon over stuffed cabbage.

Mustard-Glazed Ham

This version of a classic Southern method of treating ham made its bow in a Grey Poupon® Dijon Mustard advertisement about a dozen years ago. Great looking on a buffet table, great tasting too.

1 precooked ham, about 8 lbs. (or 5-lb. canned ham)
Whole cloves
1½ cups firmly-packed dark brown sugar
½ cup maple-flavored syrup
2 Tbs. Grey Poupon® Dijon Mustard
1 Tbs. corn starch
1 1 lb., 4-oz. can unsweetened crushed pineapple

Cut rind off ham, if present. Score top surface of ham, stud with cloves, and place, fat side up, on a rack in a shallow baking pan. Bake in a preheated oven (350°F.) approximately 15 minutes per pound, or follow wrapper directions. Combine sugar, syrup and mustard. Use ¾ cup of glaze to baste ham every 10 minutes during last 30 to 45 minutes of baking. Stir corn starch into remaining glaze in saucepan. Add pineapple with juice. Simmer, stirring constantly, until sauce thickens. Serve sauce with ham.

Golden Praline Ham

Beautiful is what you'll call this prize-winning ham recipe from Hormel.®

1 Hormel® Cure/81 Ham
1 16-oz. jar apricot-pineapple preserves
½ cup brown sugar
Pecan halves and Maraschino cherries for
garnish

Combine apricot-pineapple preserves with brown sugar and heat in saucepan, stirring well. Spread mixture over Hormel® Cure/81 Ham for last half hour of baking. When ham is finished, garnish with alternating diagonal rows of pecan halves and cherry halves.

Swiss Hamlets

The Oscar Mayer® people tell me their favorite package recipe is this easy but elegant dish. It can be put together in minutes, so you can relax and watch the evening news on TV while it bakes.

1 6 to 8 oz. package Oscar
Mayer® brand smoked
cooked ham, chopped
ham, honey loaf or
luxury loaf

4 slices Swiss cheese,
4-inches square
1 10-oz. package frozen
broccoli spears, thawed
Dill Mustard Sauce (below)

Top two slices of meat with slice of cheese and one-fourth of broccoli; roll and secure with wooden toothpicks. Place in small shallow baking dish. Repeat. Top with sauce. Bake in 350°F. oven for about 30 minutes. Remove toothpicks; serve with Dill Mustard Sauce. Makes 2 servings.

Dill Mustard Sauce

1 1-oz. package white sauce mix
¼ cup sour cream
1 Tbs. prepared mustard
¼ tsp. dill weed

Prepare white sauce according to package directions. Stir in rest of ingredients.

Spaghettini Bolognese

From the Hunt's® Tomato Paste Collection, a 1960 recipe that's still as economical to prepare (well almost) as it has been delicious to eat.

¼ lb. mushrooms, sliced
1 carrot, sliced
1 clove garlic, crushed
½ cup *each:* chopped onion, celery and green pepper
2 Tbs. pure vegetable oil
¾ lb. Italian sausage, casings removed

2 6-oz. or 1 12-oz. can Hunt's® Tomato Paste
3 cups water
¼ cup dry red wine (optional)
1 tsp. sugar
¼ tsp. Italian herb seasoning
1 lb. spaghettini, cooked and drained

Sauté mushrooms, carrot, garlic, onion, celery and green pepper in oil in Dutch oven. Add sausage; cook until sausage loses redness; drain fat. Add remaining ingredients except spaghettini. Simmer, uncovered, 30 to 40 minutes, stirring occasionally. Serve over hot spaghettini. Makes 6 to 8 servings.

Bucks County Lamb Stew

A 1930 classic from the Argo-Kingsford® Corn Starch package. Its down-home flavor has never gone out of style.

3 Tbs. corn oil
2 lbs. lamb stew meat, cut
   into 2-inch cubes
1 beef bouillon cube
2 tsps. salt
1 bay leaf
¼ tsp. crushed dried thyme
   leaves

4½ cups water
6 carrots
12 small white onions
¼ cup Argo-Kingsford's®
   Corn Starch

In skillet heat corn oil over medium heat. Add beef; brown on all sides. Add next 4 ingredients and 4 cups of the water. Cover; bring to boil. Reduce heat; simmer 1½ hours. Add carrots and onions. Simmer ½ hour or until tender. Mix Corn Starch and ½ cup water. Stir into beef mixture. Bring to boil, stirring constantly; boil 1 minute. Makes 6 servings.

Irish Stew

This recipe, from a booklet put out by the Tabasco® Hot Pepper Sauce people, was developed by James Beard. It's great tasting, but so simple to prepare any novice can do it.

3 lbs. lamb; shoulder,
   chops, breast
2 large potatoes for each
   person
2 medium onions per person
1 or 2 carrots per person

1 tsp. thyme
1 tsp. Tabasco® Hot Pepper
   Sauce
1 bay leaf
Salt to taste
Water to cover

Arrange lamb, which should have a minimum of fat, in alternating layers with potatoes, onions (thickly sliced) and carrots. Add the seasonings and just cover with water or broth. Cover and either simmer on top of the stove or cook in a 325°F. oven for 1½ to 2 hours or until meat is tender. Test for seasoning and serve with crisp bread and a good salad. Serves 4 to 6.

Veal Scaloppine al Marsala

If ever there was a dish tailor-made for quick cooking and pure enjoyment, it is this classic Italian recipe from the label of Holland House® Marsala Cooking Wine. Plain buttered noodles make a fine accompaniment.

4 veal scallops (about 1 lb., cut from leg, each about ⅛ inch thick)
Salt
Pepper
3 Tbs. butter or margarine

1 clove garlic, crushed
1 Tbs. butter or margarine
½ lb. mushrooms, sliced
½ cup Holland House® Marsala Cooking Wine

Dredge veal in flour and add salt and pepper to taste. Melt 3 Tbs. butter or margarine in skillet; brown garlic. Then add veal, browning quickly. Remove veal to shallow baking pan. Add 1 Tbs. butter to skillet and brown mushrooms. Add Holland House® Marsala Cooking Wine and bring to boil. Simmer approximately 2 minutes to blend flavors. Pour wine-mushroom sauce over veal. Cover pan and bake approximately 20 minutes at 350°F. Serves 2 to 3.

Broiled Chicken Deluxe

When Delmarva® staged their first National Chicken Cooking Contest in 1949, this recipe was the winner. It is a well thought-out method for broiling chicken, obviously by a very knowledgeable cook. You can learn quite a bit about broiling food in general just by reading the recipe. The final results cannot be improved.

1 broiler-fryer chicken, halved
½ lemon
2 tsps. salt
¼ tsp. pepper

½ tsp. paprika
½ cup butter, melted, divided
2 tsps. granulated sugar

In broiler pan place chicken skin side up. Rub surface of chicken with lemon, squeezing some juice onto meat. In bowl mix together salt, pepper and paprika. Sprinkle mixture over chicken. Brush with ½ of the butter; sprinkle with sugar. Place broiler pan as far from heat as possible and cook at 450°F. for 10 minutes allowing seasonings to penetrate. Move broiler pan up so that chicken is 3 to 6 inches from the heat in gas range or 6 to 9 inches from heat in electric range. Broil, basting frequently with remaining butter and turning to insure even browning, about 35 minutes or until fork can be inserted in chicken with ease. Makes 2 large servings.

Chicken Marseillaise

An American adaptation of a French classic and a much requested recipe from the Kraft® Kitchens.

1 2½- to 3-lb. broiler-fryer, cut up	1 tsp. salt
Kraft® Catalina French Dressing	½ tsp. celery seed
	¼ tsp. pepper
1 16-oz. can tomatoes	¼ cup wine or water
8 onion slices, ¼-inch thick	2 Tbs. flour

Brown chicken in ⅓ cup dressing over low heat. Add ¼ cup dressing, tomatoes, onion and seasonings. Cover; simmer 45 minutes. Remove chicken and vegetables to serving platter. Gradually add wine to flour, stirring until well blended. Gradually add flour mixture to hot liquid in pan; cook stirring constantly. Serve with chicken and vegetables. Makes 4 servings.

Chicken Jardiniere au Vermouth

There are many variations of this elegant French recipe, but this version from Holland House® is so easy that it's hard to believe it tastes as good as it does.

1 3-lb. broiler chicken, cut into pieces	¼ tsp. pepper
1 clove garlic, crushed	1 cup Holland House® Vermouth Cooking Wine
2 Tbs. oil	1 cup frozen peas
1 carrot	1 small can whole mushrooms
1 small zucchini	2 tsps. corn starch
1 stalk celery	
¼ tsp. thyme	

Rub chicken with garlic. Heat oil in saucepan, add chicken and brown on both sides. Add fresh vegetables (all cut into 2-inch-by-¼-inch sticks), thyme, pepper and Holland House® Cooking Wine. Stir to deglaze pan. Cover and simmer 30 minutes. Add peas and mushrooms. Stir in corn starch/water mixture. Bring to a boil, simmer 5 more minutes and serve. Makes 6 servings.

Orange Glazed Chicken

The Pompeian® Olive Oil Company considers this their best label recipe. It's the one most often used by food editors of top newspapers across the country.

½ cup Pompeian® Olive Oil
½ cup orange juice
1 Tbs. wine vinegar
1 tsp. salt
1 tsp. instant choppped
  onion
¼ tsp. ginger or cumin
1 chicken, about 3 lbs.

Combine olive oil, juice, vinegar and salt; crush the instant onion with mortar and pestle or back of wooden spoon, blend with the ginger or cumin. Add to the juice mixture. Marinate either whole or cut-up chicken in the sauce for 1 hour or longer; baste with the marinade as it cooks over charcoal or in the broiler or rotisserie oven. Makes 1 cup sauce.

Oven-Fried Chicken and Bananas

It's hard to choose favorites, but if you twisted my arm I'd have to admit that this South Seas— style dish from the inside of the label from a can of Coco Casa® Cream of Coconut is tops on my list.

2 chickens, about 3 lbs.
  each, cut up
  Salt and pepper
1 cup Coco Casa® Cream
  of Coconut

2 Tbs. lemon juice
6 medium-size bananas
2½ cups cornflake crumbs
¾ cup melted butter or
  margarine

Sprinkle chicken pieces on all sides with salt and pepper. In a bowl, mix Coco Casa® Cream of Coconut and lemon juice. Peel bananas and cut each banana into halves crosswise. Brush chicken and bananas thickly with coconut mixture and roll in crumbs, pressing firmly to make them adhere. Brush a baking pan with some of the butter. Place chicken pieces in a single layer into pan and drizzle with half of the butter. Bake in preheated 350°F. oven for 45 minutes. Add bananas and drizzle with remaining butter. Bake for another 15 minutes. Serves 6.

Oven-Fried Chicken

**One of the first and still one of the best oven-fried chicken recipes to appear on a package. It is from Pepperidge Farm®
test kitchens.**

¼ cup butter or margarine
2 cups Pepperidge Farm®
 Herb Seasoned Stuffing,
 crushed
1 tsp. salt

2- to 3-lb. chicken, cut up
1 egg
1 tablespoon water
 Gravy (below)

Preheat oven to 425°F. Put butter in shallow baking pan and place in oven until melted. Meanwhile combine crushed suffing and salt in a plastic bag. Dip chicken parts in egg that has been beaten with water. Then shake, a few pieces at a time, in bag until well coated. Place chicken, skin side down, in melted butter. Do not layer in pan. Bake, uncovered, 30 minutes, turn and continue baking for 15 minutes. Servés 4.

Gravy

1 10¾-oz. can chicken gravy
½ cup sour cream

Combine canned gravy with sour cream and heat to just below boiling.

Baked Yogurt Chicken

Love this chicken! Everyone does; it's a "most-requested" recipe at the Dannon® Yogurt kitchens.

1 cut-up frying chicken, 2½
  to 3 lbs.
  Salt and pepper
6 Tbs. butter or margarine
2 Tbs. flour
1 Tbs. paprika
2 cups Dannon® Plain
  Yogurt

¼ lb. fresh mushrooms,
  cleaned and sliced
2 Tbs. fresh lemon juice
2 Tbs. chopped fresh dill or
  parsley

Wash chicken pieces and wipe dry. Add salt and pepper. In a large pan, melt 4 Tbs. of butter; fry chicken until golden brown. Remove to buttered shallow baking dish. Sprinkle flour and paprika into pan juices and cook, stirring for 1 minute. Stir in yogurt and mix well. Spoon over chicken. Sauté mushrooms in remaining 2 Tbs. of butter and lemon juice for 1 minute and spoon over pan. Sprinkle with the dill. Bake, covered, in preheated moderate oven (325°F.) for about 1¼ hours, or until chicken is tender. Serves about 4.

Sweet 'N' Smoky
Oven-Barbecued Chicken

This chicken recipe is still as great as it was in 1966 when it won top place at the Delmarva® National Chicken Cooking Contest. The delicious flavor comes from a master-blend glaze of catsup, mustard, oil, vinegar and maple syrup— delicious!!

1 broiler-fryer chicken, cut
   in serving pieces
½ cup of water
1 large onion, sliced
1 tsp. hickory-smoked salt
¼ tsp. pepper
   Barbecue Sauce (below)

Place chicken, skin side up, in baking pan. Pour water around chicken. Tuck onion slices in and around the chicken. Sprinkle with hickory smoked salt and pepper. Bake chicken, uncovered, for 30 minutes in 375°F. oven. Mix catsup and mustard, add oil, vinegar and maple syrup. Pour Barbecue Sauce over chicken and bake 30 minutes longer, or until fork can be inserted in chicken with ease. Makes 4 servings.

Barbecue Sauce

½ cup catsup
2 Tbs. prepared mustard
½ cup cooking oil
¼ cup vinegar
½ cup maple syrup

Combine above ingredients.

Chicken Argentina

The California Olive Industry used this recipe in a national advertising campaign. The resulting fan letters were enthusiastic to say the least. "Delicate and unique," "light and elegant," "just great," "superb," they wrote. After testing, I agree—it's all that and more.

1 frying chicken (3 lbs.),	¼ cup oil
cut in pieces	1 large onion, chopped
1 lime	1 medium green pepper,
1 tsp. salt	sliced
½ tsp. pepper	1 medium red pepper,
¾ tsp. paprika	sliced
1½ cups pitted California	1½ cups orange juice
ripe olives	

Marinate chicken pieces in juice from the lime (approximately ⅓ cup) for at least 30 minutes. Combine salt, pepper and paprika; sprinkle over chicken. Brown on all sides in oil. Place chicken in baking pan, add olives, onion, green pepper, red pepper and orange juice. Cover and bake at 350°F. for 45 minutes or until chicken is tender. Remove chicken to platter. Serve with pan juices. Serves 4.

Pettengill Schoolhouse Chicken Pie

Here is a recipe usually sent to consumers who write the Argo-Kingsford® Corn Starch kitchens requesting "something real good to take to a covered dish supper," and it is *real good*!

2 Tbs. margarine	2 cups fresh peas, cooked
1 cup sliced mushrooms	1 whole pimiento, chopped
1 clove garlic, minced	½ tsp. dried thyme leaves
2 Tbs. Argo-Kingsford's®	1 tsp. salt
Corn Starch	¼ tsp. pepper
1½ cups milk	1 recipe double-crust pastry
2½ cups cooked chicken, cut	
into bite-size pieces	

In skillet melt margarine. Add mushrooms and garlic. Sauté over medium heat until lightly browned. In saucepan stir together Corn Starch and milk until smooth. Mix in mushrooms, garlic and pan drippings. Bring to a boil over medium heat, stirring constantly, and boil 1 minute. Stir in next 6 ingredients. Pour into pastry-lined 9-inch pie plate. Cover pie with pastry; seal and flute edge. Cut slits in top. Bake in 375°F. oven 35 minutes or until crust is golden brown. Serves 6 to 8.

Country-Style Chicken Kiev

Land O Lakes® printed this easy, elegant chicken recipe on their unsalted butter package. It has been voted one of their best by the executive staff.

½ cup fine dry bread crumbs
2 Tbs. grated Parmesan cheese
1 tsp. *each* basil leaves and oregano leaves
½ tsp. garlic salt
¼ tsp. salt
⅔ cup Land O Lakes® Sweet Cream Butter, melted

2 chicken breasts, split (about 1½ lbs.)
¼ cup white wine or apple juice
¼ cup chopped green onion
¼ cup chopped fresh parsley

Heat oven to 375°F. Combine bread crumbs, Parmesan cheese, basil, oregano, garlic salt and salt. Dip chicken breasts in melted Butter, then coat with crumb mixture; *reserve* remaining butter. Place chicken skin side up in ungreased 9-inch square baking dish. Bake for 50 to 60 minutes or until chicken is fork tender. Meanwhile, add wine, green onion and parsley to reserved melted butter (about ½ cup). When chicken is golden brown, pour butter sauce over chicken. Continue baking for 3 to 5 minutes or until sauce is heated through. Serve with sauce spooned over. Makes 4 servings.

Indian Chicken Curry

This recipe from a Coco Casa® Cream of Coconut label is as authentic a curry dish as any you are apt to find this side of New Delhi.

⅓ cup butter or margarine
1 large onion, chopped
1 cup chopped celery
2 tart apples, peeled and chopped
1 Tbs. curry powder
6 Tbs. flour

1 cup chicken broth
½ cup Coco Casa® Cream of Coconut
2 cups (1 pint) half-and-half
3 cups diced cooked chicken, turkey or lamb
Salt and pepper

In a large saucepan, melt butter and sauté onion, celery and apples for 5 minutes. Stir in curry and flour. Gradually stir in chicken broth, cream of coconut and half-and-half. Stir over moderate heat until sauce bubbles and thickens. Stir in chicken and season to taste with salt and pepper. Serve spooned over rice. Makes 6 to 8 servings.

Glazed Turkey Roast

A new recipe using thrifty frozen turkey loaf—a gift from Pepperidge Farm.® So good, it's destined to becme a classic.

Turkey roast*
Apricot jam or preserves
1 cup dried apricots
1 cup water
1 Tbs. brown sugar
1 Tbs. lemon juice

½ cup butter or margarine
1 8-oz. package Pepperidge Farm® Herb Seasoned Cube Stuffing
½ cup slivered almonds
¼ tsp. salt

* Turkey roasts vary from 2 to 4½ lbs. in size. They can be all white meat or a combination of white and dark. Some come with prepared gravy. For best results use a meat thermometer and roast to 185°F. Let stand 10 minutes before slicing. Allow ⅓-lb. meat for each serving.

Roast turkey according to package directions. For glaze, brush top of the roast with apricot jam frequently during the last 30 minutes. Meanwhile place the apricots, water, brown sugar and lemon juice in a small saucepan and simmer for 5 minutes. Drain, reserving the liquid. Add water to liquid to make 1 cup. Place in a large saucepan with butter and heat until butter is melted. Stir in stuffing, almonds and salt. Cut apricots in strips and add to mixture. Place in a 1-quart baking dish and bake alongside of turkey for the last 25 minutes. To serve: make a bed of dressing on a hot platter and place roast on top.

Mexican Turkey Bake

Were you looking for another way to use that leftover turkey? This one was found in a neat little give-away folder of recipes in a box of Uncle Ben's Converted® Brand Rice. It proved to be the most popular dish in that folder and no wonder. I tried it and it was a real success.

1 cup Uncle Ben's Con-
verted® Brand Rice
1 can (about 3 ozs.) mild
green chilies, drained
and chopped
3 cups cubed cooked tur-
key

1 12-oz. can Mexican-style
corn with sweet pep-
pers, drained
1 10-oz. can enchilada
sauce
¾ tsp. salt
1 cup dairy sour cream

Prepare rice according to package directions. Reserve 1 Tbs. chilies for garnish. Combine remaining chilies, turkey, corn, enchilada sauce, salt and cooked rice in large bowl. Spoon into greased baking dish 12 × 7½ × 2 inches. Cover and bake at 350°F. until hot, about 25 minutes. Spoon sour cream down center; garnish with reserved chilies. Makes 6 servings.

Polynesian Turkey and Noodles

Mueller's® developed this really great and different-tasting recipe to make good use of leftover turkey.

2 cups cubed cooked
turkey
1 egg, slightly beaten
¼ cup corn starch
2 Tbs. cooking oil
1 13½-oz. can pineapple
chunks, drained (reserve
juice)
½ cup sugar
½ cup cider vinegar

1 medium green pepper,
cut in strips
2 Tbs. corn starch
¼ cup water
1 tsp. soy sauce
4 large carrots, cooked and
cut in 1-inch pieces
8 oz. (5 cups) Mueller's®
Klops® Egg Noodles

Dip turkey pieces in egg; roll in ¼ cup corn starch until coated. In skillet, brown turkey pieces in oil; remove and set aside. Add enough water to reserved pineapple juice to make 1 cup; add to skillet along with sugar, vinegar and green pepper. Heat to boiling, stirring constantly. Reduce heat; cover and simmer 2 minutes. Blend 2 Tbs. corn starch and ¼ cup water; stir into skillet. Heat, stirring constantly, until mixture thickens and boils; cook 1 minute. Stir in pineapple chunks, soy sauce, carrots and turkey pieces; heat. Meanwhile, cook Egg Noodles as directed on package; drain. Serve turkey over noodles. Makes 4 to 6 servings.

Old-Fashioned Turkey Stuffing and Variations

It's on the package, it's *always* been on the package and I guess it will always *be* on the package. Good cooks have relied on this recipe from Pepperidge Farm® for twenty years.

I highly recommend the Giblet variation—it's the one my mother used every Thanksgiving Day for as far back as I can remember.

¾ cup chopped onion
1 cup chopped celery
1 cup butter or margarine
2 cups water

1 1-lb. package Pepperidge Farm® Herb-Seasoned Stuffing

In a large saucepan, sauté the onion and celery in butter until tender but not browned. Stir in water and then stuffing. Makes enough to fill a 12- to 16-lb turkey.

Variations: Try the following with a 1-lb. bag of herb-seasoned stuffing, prepared according to package directions:

Parsley
1 cup chopped parsley, ¾ cup chopped onion and 1 cup chopped celery sautéed in 1 cup butter.

Oriental
¼ cup chopped onion, ½ cup chopped celery, 1 cup sliced mushrooms and ½ cup sliced water chestnuts sautéed in 1 cup butter.

Nut
1 cup chopped celery, ½ cup onion and 1 cup nuts sautéed in 1 cup butter. Almonds, Brazil nuts, chestnuts, filberts, pecans or walnuts may be used.

Giblet
Simmer turkey giblets with seasonings 2 to 3 hours. Remove liver after 10 to 20 minutes. Drain, reserving broth;

chop coarsely. Sauté ¾ cup chopped onion and 1 cup chopped celery in 1 cup butter. Use reserved broth in place of water in recipe. Stir chopped giblets and liver into stuffing.

Fish Fillets Sauterne

This may well have been the first recipe your mother (or grandmother) ever prepared with wine. It first appeared in 1935 on the back label of a bottle of Regina® Cooking Sauterne. I still use it, often adding my own touch—a sprinkling of slivered almonds sautéed in butter until golden.

 ¼ cup butter
 ½ cup Regina® Cooking Sauterne
 ⅛ tsp. pepper
 1 Tbs. dried parsley flakes
 2 lb. white fish fillets (sole, flounder, haddock)

Melt butter in large skillet. Stir in Sauterne, pepper and parsley. Place fish in pan. Spoon sauce over fish. Simmer, covered, 5 to 10 minutes or until fish flakes easily with a fork. Remove fish to warm platter. Boil sauce until slightly thickened. Spoon sauce over fish. Serves 6.

Sole in Almond Shrimp Sauce

This entrée, in a velvety sauce garnished with tiny coral shrimp and golden almonds, makes a truly memorable meal.

It's one of the most popular from the permanent files at the Blue Diamond® Almonds test kitchens.

1 to 1½ lbs. sole fillets
1 cup dry white wine
3 ozs. cooked baby shrimp
4 Tbs. butter
2 Tbs. all-purpose flour
½ cup half-and-half

¼ tsp. salt
Dash pepper
⅓ cup Blue Diamond®
   Blanched Slivered
   Almonds, toasted

Poach fillets in wine in 350°F. oven until fish flakes easily with fork, but is still moist, 15 to 20 minutes. *Do not overcook.* Reserve ¼ cup shrimp; mash remaining with 2 Tbs. butter; set aside. In small saucepan, heat 2 remaining Tbs. butter. Add flour; cook 2 to 3 minutes. Gradually stir in half-and-half. Cook and stir over medium heat until sauce begins to thicken. Stir in ½ cup of fish cooking liquid; continue cooking and stirring until sauce boils. Reduce heat, add shrimp butter, salt and pepper; stir until butter melts. Stir in ¼ cup of the almonds. Arrange fillets on serving platter. Pour sauce over; garnish with remaining shrimp and almonds. Makes 4 servings.

Creole Snapper

A Creole dish from the Kikkoman® test kitchens that proves you don't have to be Creole to develop a terrific Louisiana-style baked fish recipe.

2 lbs. fresh or frozen red
   snapper fillets (thawed, if
   frozen)
6 Tbs. Kikkoman® Teriyaki
   Sauce, divided
4 Tbs. lemon juice, divided
1 Tbs. vegetable oil

½ cup diced celery
½ cup diced green pepper
½ cup diced onion
¼ tsp. Tabasco® Pepper
   Sauce
1 cup diced tomatoes

Cut fish fillets into serving portions; drain thoroughly on paper towels. Combine 4 Tbs. Kikkoman® Teriyaki Sauce and 1 Tbs. lemon juice in large shallow pan. Arrange fish, in single layer, in sauce; marinate 15 minutes, turning over once. Bake fish in sauce in preheated 350°F. oven 12 to 15 minutes, or until fish flakes easily with fork. Meanwhile, heat oil in large frying pan. Add celery, green pepper and onion and sauté over medium heat until tender, yet crisp. Stir in remaining 2 Tbs. Teriyaki Sauce, 3 Tbs. lemon juice and pepper sauce; bring to boil. Add tomatoes and cook only until heated through, stirring constantly. To serve, remove fish from sauce; top with tomato mixture and serve immediately. Makes 6 servings.

Fillets Baked in Sour Cream

This is the sophisticated kind of dish you'd expect to find in an expensive French restaurant, but it's surprisingly easy to prepare. A 4-star favorite ever since it was printed about 10 years ago in a booklet on "The Art Of Seasoning" prepared by the Tabasco® Hot Pepper Sauce test kitchens.

4 tsps. butter or margarine, divided
2 lbs. fish fillets (sole, haddock or flounder)
1 tsp. salt
½ tsp. Tabasco® Hot Pepper Sauce

1 Tbs. paprika
¼ cup grated Parmesan cheese
1 cup (8 ozs.) sour cream
¼ cup fine dry bread crumbs

Grease 2-quart baking dish with 1 tsp. of the butter. Arrange fish in baking dish. Blend salt, Tabasco® Hot Pepper Sauce, paprika and Parmesan cheese into sour cream. Spread over fish. Top with bread crumbs and dot with remaining 3 tsps. butter. Bake, uncovered, in 350°F. oven 30 minutes until fish is easily flaked with a fork. Serve with lemon slices, if desired. Makes 4 to 6 servings.

Baked Fish Fillets José

Baked fish takes on a Mexican flavor when you follow the directions on the label of the Ortega® Taco Dinner package.

1 7-oz. package Ortega® Taco Dinner (Shells,
    Seasoning and Sauce)
2 lbs. fish fillets
½ cup butter (or margarine), melted

Heat Taco Shells according to package directions. In food processor or blender, finely crush shells. Blend in Taco Seasoning. Dip fish in butter. Coat with crumbs. Arrange in shallow baking dish. Bake in preheated 425°F. oven 15 to 20 minutes or until fish flakes easily with a fork. Serve with Ortega® Taco Sauce. Makes 6 servings.

Tuna Shortcake

This is one of America's "stand by" Campbell's® Soup recipes. Try it as a 4 A.M. breakfast after a night of serious partying or as a 1 P.M. brunch the next day. It's a hot lunch for the young set or a light supper dish for an "I hate to cook" night. It's one of those "add a" recipes—add a dash of white wine, a can of sliced mushrooms, a handful of slivered almonds—and serve on cornbread squares, English muffins or what have you.

1 can Campbell's® Cream of Chicken Soup
¼ cup milk
1 7-oz. can tuna, drained and flaked
1 cup cooked peas
1 Tbs. chopped pimiento

In saucepan, combine ingredients. Heat; stir often. Serve over biscuits. Makes about 2½ cups.

Tuna Pie

**One of the first recipes used to introduce Pepperidge Farm®
Frozen Patty Shells. A step up from tuna salad sandwiches,
wouldn't you say?**

2 Tbs. butter or margarine
½ cup slivered almonds
2 6½-oz. cans tuna, drained
1 16-oz. can cut green
   beans, drained
1 6-oz. can sliced
   mushrooms, drained
2 10½-oz. cans condensed
   cream of mushroom soup,
   undiluted

⅓ cup sherry
1 10-oz. package
   Pepperidge Farm® frozen
   Patty Shells
1 egg, well beaten

Thaw package of Patty Shells in refrigerator overnight or on a kitchen counter until workable, always keeping them cold to the touch. In a skillet, heat butter and sauté almonds until golden. Stir in tuna, green beans, mushrooms, soup and sherry. Pour mixture into a shallow 1½-quart casserole. Stack 3 Patty Shells one atop the other. On a lightly floured surface roll out to about 4 × 9 inches. With a cookie cutter cut pastry into 2-inch rounds. Repeat with remaining Patty Shells. Place rounds on a cookie sheet and brush tops with beaten egg. Bake casserole and pastry rounds in 400°F. oven for 15 to 20 minutes or until rounds are puffed and brown. Place puff pastry rounds over the top of the tuna casserole. Serve at once. Serves 6.

Salmon Sour Cream Puffs

Borden® Sour Cream sponsored a national recipe contest back in the 1970's and out of 10,000 recipes entered, 14 were selected and appeared in a booklet called "Award Winning Recipes made with Borden® Sour Cream." This one won second prize.

1 15½-oz. can salmon, drained
1½ cups soft bread crumbs (about 4 slices)
1 8-oz. container Borden® Sour Cream
2 eggs, separated
2 Tbs. chopped chives
¼ tsp. salt
Dash pepper
1 to 1¼ cups finely chopped almonds
Vegetable oil
Lemon wedges

Remove skin and bones from salmon. In large bowl, combine salmon, crumbs, Borden® Sour Cream, egg yolks, chives, salt and pepper; mix well. Beat egg whites until stiff; fold into salmon mixture. On large sheet of wax paper, sprinkle half the almonds. Drop heaping tablespoonfuls of salmon mixture onto almonds; sprinkle remaining almonds over top. In large skillet, heat oil; lift puffs with spatula into skillet. Brown on each side. Serve hot with lemon wedges. Refrigerate leftovers. Makes 6 servings.

Szechuan Shrimp

Based on a dish served in a famous New York Chinese restaurant, this recipe appeared in a Planters® Peanut Oil ad in the late 1970's. It is pleasantly hot with a touch of sweetness—an authentic Szechuan-style dish.

½ cup minced bamboo
shoots
½ cup minced scallions
¼ tsp. minced fresh ginger
root
3 large cloves garlic,
minced
¼ tsp. liquid hot pepper
sauce
2 Tbs. sugar
½ cup catsup

3 Tbs. Dry Sack® Sherry
1 Tbs. soy sauce
1½ tsps. sesame oil or 1 Tbs.
toasted sesame seeds
1 Tbs. corn starch
3 Tbs. water
1½ cups Planters® Peanut
Oil
1 lb. shelled and deveined
raw shrimp

Combine bamboo shoots, scallions, ginger, garlic and red pepper sauce in a small bowl. In second bowl combine sugar, catsup, Dry Sack Sherry, soy sauce and sesame oil or seeds. In third bowl mix corn starch and water. Heat Planters® Peanut Oil in wok or large skillet to 400°F. Have ready a large strainer with a bowl underneath. Add shrimp to hot oil, stirring until done, about 2 minutes. Pour oil and shrimp into strainer to drain. Heat 2 Tbs. of the strained oil in same wok or skillet over high heat. Add scallion mixture and stir-fry 1 minute. Add drained shrimp and continue to stir-fry 30 seconds. Pour in catsup mixture. Cook stirring, 30 seconds. Blend corn starch and water and add to wok. Cook and stir until slightly thickened. Serves 4.

Crisco's® French-Fried Butterfly Shrimp

Simply spectacular and not in the least difficult to prepare. For a great, almost no-work menu, serve hot shrimp with made-ahead coleslaw and canned shoestring potatoes.

2 lbs. shelled, deveined
   shrimp
1 cup sifted all-purpose
   enriched flour
½ tsp. sugar
½ tsp. salt

1 cup ice water
2 Tbs. Crisco® Oil
1 egg
   Crisco® Oil for deep frying
   Hot sauce

With a sharp knife slit shrimp deeply down back without cutting all the way through. Wash shrimp and dry between paper towels. In a bowl, combine flour, sugar and salt. Add ice water, 2 Tbs. Crisco® Oil and the egg; beat until smooth. Dip shrimp, a few at a time, into the mixture. Fry in deep Crisco® Oil heated to 375°F. Cook for 3 to 5 minutes, until golden brown. Drain on paper towels. Serve hot with your favorite hot sauce. Makes 6 servings.

The Luxury Liner

It's no shrimp boat! Built by Holland House® Wine and California avocados, it is indeed a luxury liner.

2 Tbs. butter
½ cup onion, finely chopped
1 cup zucchini, finely diced
½ cup Holland House®
   Sherry Cooking Wine
½ cup water
2 Tbs. tomato sauce or 1 ripe
   tomato, chopped
1 chicken-flavor bouillon cube

½ lb. medium-size fresh or
   frozen shrimp,* shelled
   and deveined
1 Tbs. corn starch, dissolved
   in 2 Tbs. cold water
1 Tbs. bread crumbs
3 California avocados,
   halved, pitted and peeled

*Chicken breast cut into ¼-inch cubes may be substituted.

Melt butter in saucepan. Add onion and zucchini and cook 5 minutes over medium heat. Stir in sherry, water, bouillon cube and tomato. Cook 3 minutes over high heat. Add shrimp and cook, stirring, about 1 minute until shrimp turn pink. Add corn starch mixture and cook, stirring, until mixture comes to boil. Remove from heat. Place avocado halves on baking dish. Fill each half with shrimp mixture, spooning remainder of sauce around them. Sprinkle with crumbs and broil 1 to 2 minutes until crumbs brown. Serve immediately, as an appetizer for 6 or luncheon entrée for 3.

Classic Crab Newburg

Here is the recipe most Americans use when preparing this adaptation of a lobster dish created at New York's famed Delmonico Restaurant during the Gay Nineties. It's on the Wakefield® Snow Crabmeat package and has been as long as I can remember.

1 6-oz. package
    Wakefield® Snow
    Crabmeat
¼ cup butter
2 Tbs. flour
½ tsp. salt
⅛ tsp. nutmeg

⅛ tsp. cayenne
2 cups half-and-half or
    light cream
3 egg yolks, slightly beaten
1½ Tbs. dry sherry
Hot, cooked rice

Thaw and drain Crabmeat. Melt butter in medium saucepan. Add flour, salt, nutmeg and cayenne. Stir until smooth. Gradually add half-and-half. Cook over medium heat 8 to 10 minutes or until slightly thickened, stirring constantly. Gradually add ½ cup hot sauce mixture to egg yolks, beating to blend. Add egg yolk mixture to remaining sauce mixture; mix well. Add crab and crab liquid. Cook 1 to 2 minutes or until thickened, stirring constantly. Remove from heat. Stir in sherry. Serve over hot, cooked rice. Serves 4 to 5.

Crab Louis

After much reviewing and reminiscing, the Campbell® Soup test kitchens selected this recipe as one of the all-time best from their extensive files.

1 10¾ oz. can Campbell's®
  Condensed Cream of
  Celery Soup
½ cup chili sauce
¼ cup mayonnaise
2 Tbs. finely chopped onion
  Generous dash pepper

¼ cup heavy cream,
  whipped
4 cups cooked flaked crab
  meat (about 1½ lbs.)
  Hard-cooked egg, cut in
  wedges
  Tomatoes, cut in wedges

Blend Soup, chili sauce, mayonnaise, onion and pepper; fold in whipped cream. Add crab; chill. Place crab on bed of lettuce. Garnish with egg and tomato. Makes about 4 cups.

Deviled Seafood

One of the simplest and nicest party dishes is this one from the Pepperidge Farm® test kitchens. If you don't already have it (it was first printed 8 years ago), you most certainly should.

¼ cup finely chopped
  green pepper
¼ cup finely chopped onion
1 cup finely chopped celery
1 tsp. Worcestershire sauce
½ tsp. salt
1 6- to 7-oz. can shrimp,
  drained

1 6- to 7-oz. can crab meat,
  flaked
2 cups Pepperidge Farm®
  Herb-Seasoned Stuffing,
  crushed
1 cup mayonnaise

Stir together all ingredients until blended. Spoon into a 1-quart shallow casserole or 8 oven-proof shells. Bake at 350°F. for 30 minutes or until lightly browned. Serves 6 to 8.

Creamy Mustard Sauce

This classic, positively superb, old English sauce recipe has been on the sides of Colman's Dry Mustard cans for almost 30 years. A positive "must" for every good cook's file.

2 to 3 tsps. Colman's®
 Mustard (dry)
2 to 3 tsps. water
¼ cup vinegar
1 cup heavy cream

½ cup beef bouillon
1 Tbs. corn starch
¼ tsp. salt
1 Tbs. butter

Combine Colman's Mustard and water; let stand 10 minutes. Boil vinegar in small saucepan until reduced to 1 Tbs. Stir in heavy cream, bouillon, corn starch and salt. Cook and stir until thickened. Add butter and mustard mixture. Serve with beef, pork, lamb and vegetables.

Basic Bordelaise Sauce

This recipe from the permanent file at Holland House® test kitchens will leave guests thinking you spent hours at the stove.

3 Tbs. butter
¼ cup diced onions
2 Tbs. flour
1 cup beef bouillon

½ cup Holland House® Red
 Cooking Wine
1 Tbs. chopped parsley
1 clove garlic, crushed

Heat butter in large skillet. Sauté onions in butter until golden; add flour and blend thoroughly. Add bouillon and stir until smooth. Blend in Holland House® Red Cooking Wine, parsley and garlic. Delicious on steak, roast beef and chops.

Creole Sauce

Louisiana housewives used to spend a whole day preparing Creole Sauce. Heinz® test-kitchen cooks make it quick, simple and simply delicious with this easy recipe.

1 large onion, thinly sliced	½ cup water
¼ cup chopped green pepper	1 Tbs. Heinz® Worcestershire Sauce
2 Tbs. butter or margarine	½ tsp. salt
½ cup Heinz® Tomato Ketchup	Dash pepper

In saucepan, sauté onion and green pepper in butter until tender. Stir in ketchup, water, Worcestershire Sauce, salt and pepper. Simmer, uncovered, 10 minutes, stirring occasionally. Serve over baked, broiled or fried fish, omelets or other meat or chicken dishes. Makes 1½ cups sauce.

Slimmed-Down Pasta Sauce

For weight-watchers who are also pasta lovers, this sauce is the answer to a prayer; an extremely popular recipe from Mueller's.®

1 24-oz. can tomato juice
1 6-oz. can tomato paste
½ cup grated carrot
2 large cloves garlic,
   mashed
1 tsp. oregano leaves,
   crushed
1 tsp. onion salt
1 medium bay leaf
   Dash pepper

To make basic sauce, combine all ingredients in sauce-pan. Simmer 30 minutes, stirring occasionally. Remove bay leaf. Makes about 3½ cups sauce (300 calories total).

Variations:

Ground Beef: In saucepan brown ½ lb. lean ground beef (10% fat); add basic sauce ingredients and proceed as directed. Makes about 4⅓ cups sauce.

Mushroom: Add 1 cup sliced fresh mushrooms, or a 4-oz. can sliced mushrooms (with liquid) to basic sauce ingredients; proceed as directed. Makes about 4⅔ cups sauce.

Easy Meat Sauce

Lipton® featured this quick spaghetti sauce on their Onion Soup Mix package back in the 1960's. It was popular then and is even more so today.

1 lb. ground beef
1 clove garlic, finely chopped
1 envelope Lipton® Onion Soup mix
¼ tsp. oregano
1 28-oz. can tomato puree
1 cup water

In large saucepan, brown ground beef with garlic; stir in Lipton® Onion Soup mix, oregano, tomato puree and wa-ter. Simmer covered, stirring occasionally, about 30 minutes. Serve over hot noodles, spaghetti or rice. Makes about 5 cups sauce.

San Clemente Ham Sauce

The great cooks at the Sun-Maid® test kitchen tell me this is their all-time favorite sauce recipe.

½ cup Sun-Maid® Seed-less Raisins
½ cup Sun-Maid® Golden Seedless Raisins
¼ cup brown sugar
1½ Tbs. corn starch
¼ tsp. salt
½ tsp. dry mustard

Generous dash cloves
2 Tbs. vinegar
2 Tbs. ham drippings or butter
1 cup water
½ cup orange or pineapple juice
¼ cup Chablis

Bring all ingredients to a boil and simmer 5 minutes. Makes 2 cups sauce.

Cranberry Wine Sauce

Armour® put this American original on their Gold Star Boneless Turkey label a few years ago. It's superb.

1 16-oz. can whole berry cranberry sauce
¼ cup Burgundy wine
2 Tbs. brown sugar, packed
1 Tbs. prepared mustard
¼ tsp. onion salt

In saucepan, combine all ingredients. Simmer, uncovered, 5 minutes. Serve warm with sliced turkey. To serve with cold sliced turkey, chill sauce and spoon over turkey. Makes 2½ cups.

Basic Newburg Sauce

This is a basic cream-based sauce from the label of Holland House® Cooking Sherry that has so many uses it just can't be left out of this book. Serve it over shrimp or lobster as suggested below, or try it served over vegetables, leftover turkey or chicken, or use it instead of Hollandaise for Eggs Benedict—all lovely ideas, each as good as the other.

2 Tbs. butter
1 Tbs. flour
1 cup heavy cream
1 egg yolk
   Salt and pepper to taste
2 Tbs. Holland House®
   Sherry Cooking Wine

Heat butter in large skillet. Sprinkle flour into butter and blend thoroughly. Gradually add heavy cream to mixture and cook, stirring constantly until thick and smooth (do not boil). Pour mixture over well-beaten egg yolk, stirring constantly with spoon or whisk. Salt and pepper to taste.

For Seafood Newburg:

Add to Newburg sauce 1 lb. cooked shrimp or lobster meat, seasoned by tossing with 2 Tbs. Holland House® Sherry Cooking Wine. Heat through and serve over rice or toast. Makes 4 average servings.
Cook over boiling water for 1 to 2 minutes, stirring constantly. Stir in cooking wine.

Basic Barbecue Sauce

A classic for sure. This simple, but very versatile and utterly delicious sauce recipe has been featured on the Grandma's® Molasses label for over 10 years.

1 cup Grandma's® Molasses
1 cup prepared mustard
1 cup vinegar

Mix molasses and mustard; stir in vinegar. Cover and refrigerate. Makes 3 cups.

Variations:

Tomato Barbecue Sauce: Add 1 cup catsup to Basic Barbecue Sauce. Yields 1 quart.

Herb Barbecue Sauce: Add ¼ tsp. each, marjoram, oregano and thyme to 1 cup Basic Barbecue Sauce. Yields 1 cup.

For Oven-Broiled Chicken: Brush sauce on chicken parts, broil until tender, brush again.

For Barbecue Hamburger: Flavor, knead sauce into meat, brush on burgers, brown.

For Baked Glazed Ham: Brush with sauce during last half-hour of baking.

Lipton® Onion Butter

The Lipton® people printed this "terrific-idea" recipe on their Onion Soup mix packages years ago. It has become a classic, so don't wait—make it up today to have on hand when you want to make something especially good.

1 envelope Lipton® Onion Soup mix
1 8-oz. container whipped butter, or
½ lb. butter or margarine, softened

Thoroughly blend Lipton® Onion Soup mix with butter. Store covered in refrigerator. Makes about 1¼ cups.

Onion-Buttered Bread: Spread Onion Butter between slices of French or Italian bread; wrap in foil and heat in 375°F. oven 15 to 20 minutes.

Onion-Buttered Baked Potatoes: Top a hot, split baked potato with 1 to 2 Tbs. Onion Butter.

Onion-Buttered Whipped Potatoes: Add ¼ cup Onion Butter and ¼ cup milk to 4 medium-cooked potatoes; beat until light and fluffy.

For Instant Potatoes: Prepare instant mashed potatoes according to package directions, using twice as much Onion Butter for butter.

Onion-Buttered Noodles: Toss ½ lb. cooked and drained noodles with ¼ cup Onion Butter.

Onion-Buttered Vegetables: Add 2 Tbs. Onion Butter to a cooked and drained 10-oz. package frozen vegetable.

Onion-Buttered Corn-on-the-Cob: Spread Onion Butter on hot cooked ears of corn; or spread on uncooked corn, then wrap in foil and toast on outdoor grill or in 400°F. oven about 30 minutes.

Onion-Buttered Sandwiches: Use softened Onion Butter to spread on bread slices when making sandwiches. Especially good with roast beef, cheese, lettuce and tomatoes.

Onion-Buttered Popcorn: Toss 2½ quarts popped popcorn with ½ cup melted Onion Butter.

Onion-Buttered Crescents: Separate one 8-oz. package refrigerated crescent dinner rolls into 8 triangles. Spread with Onion Butter. Roll up and bake according to package directions.

Macaroni & Beans Italiano

This is a hearty dish, the kind I like to serve on a cold winter night. It's a meatless recipe that meat lovers will love when some crusty homemade bread is served on the side. From the Heinz permanent file of "most-often-requested."

½ cup chopped onion
½ cup chopped green pepper
1 medium zucchini, cut into ⅛-inch slices
3 Tbs. margarine or olive oil
¾ cup Heinz® Tomato Ketchup
¾ cup water

1 tsp. salt
½ tsp. oregano leaves
¼ tsp. garlic salt
⅛ tsp. pepper
1 1-lb. can Heinz® Vegetarian Beans in Tomato Sauce
1½ cups cooked macaroni
Grated Parmesan cheese

Sauté first 3 ingredients in margarine until tender. Stir in ketchup and next 5 ingredients. Combine with beans and macaroni in a 1½-quart casserole. Bake in 375°F. oven, 35 to 40 minutes. Stir occasionally. Serve with Parmesan cheese. Makes 4 to 5 servings (about 4½ cups).

At-Ease Macaroni and Cheese

An "Elsie extra" from Borden's®—old-fashioned (remember how you loved it?) macaroni and cheese. This version is made especially good with sour cream.

2 Tbs. Borden® Country Store Butter
2 Tbs. flour
½ tsp. salt
Dash pepper
½ cup Borden® Milk
1½ cups (6 ozs.) shredded Cheddar cheese

1 8-oz. container Borden® Sour Cream
1 cup uncooked macaroni, cooked and drained (2 cups cooked)

In medium saucepan, melt Butter; blend in flour, salt and pepper. Gradually stir in Milk and cheese; cook and stir over medium heat until thickened and smooth. Stir in Sour Cream and macaroni; heat through (do not boil). Garnish as desired. Refrigerate leftovers. Makes 4 to 6 servings.

Spinach Fettucine

Here's a delicious spin-off from classic Fettucine Alfredo adapted by the good cooks at Mueller's® test kitchens. A meatless main-course recipe, it is currently very popular and destined to remain so.

½ lb. fresh spinach
1 clove garlic, mashed
2 Tbs. chopped onion
½ cup butter or margarine
8 ozs. (5½ to 6 cups) Mueller's® Medium Egg Noodles

½ cup heavy cream
1 cup grated Parmesan cheese
Pepper

Remove and discard tough stems from spinach; tear or coarsely chop leaves. In pan, cook garlic and onion in half the butter until golden. Add spinach; cover and cook until just wilted. Meanwhile, cook noodles as directed on package; drain and mix with remaining butter. Then toss with cream, cheese and spinach. Pass the pepper mill or shaker. Makes 3 to 4 servings.

Fettucine Romano

Here is one of the easiest pasta recipes you will ever find and one of the most delicious. An Italian classic perfected at the Hunt-Wesson® test kitchens.

8 ozs. fettucine or wide egg
  noodles
  Boiling salted water
½ cup finely chopped onion
¼ cup butter
 1 6-oz. can Hunt's® Tomato
  Paste

 2 cups water
¼ cup grated Romano or
  Parmesan cheese
½ cup sour cream
¼ cup chopped fresh parsley

Cook fettucine in boiling, salted water until tender; drain well. Meanwhile, sauté onion in butter. Thoroughly blend in Hunt's Tomato Paste and water; heat through. Pour over hot cooked fettucine and toss with Romano cheese. Fold in sour cream. Sprinkle with parsley. Makes 4 to 6 servings.

Layered Spinach Supreme

One of the first of the "no-time-to-cook" recipes from Bisquick.® It's still considered by most cooks to be one of the best.

1 cup Bisquick® Baking Mix
¼ cup milk
2 eggs
¼ cup finely chopped onion
1 10-oz. package frozen chopped spinach, thawed and drained
½ cup grated Parmesan cheese

4 ozs. Monterey Jack cheese, cut into about ½-inch cubes
1 12-oz. carton cottage cheese
½ tsp. salt
2 cloves garlic, crushed
2 eggs

Heat oven to 375°F. Grease rectangular baking dish, 12 × 7½ × 2 inches. Mix Bisquick® Baking Mix, milk, 2 eggs and the onion; beat vigorously 20 strokes. Spread in dish. Mix remaining ingredients; spoon evenly over batter in dish. Bake until set, about 30 minutes. Let stand 5 minutes before cutting. Makes 6 to 8 servings.

Gourmet French Omelet

One of my own favorite omelets. It's quick to prepare and makes a light but satisfying meal any time of day or night. A Kraft® specialty.

2 2½-oz. jars sliced mushrooms, drained
3 Tbs. Parkay® Margarine
6 eggs, beaten
⅓ cup milk
   Salt and pepper

¾ cup (3 ozs.) shredded Cracker Barrel® Brand Sharp Natural Cheddar Cheese
1 tsp. finely chopped chives

Sauté mushrooms in 1 Tbs. Margarine. Melt remaining margarine in 10-inch skillet over low heat. Combine eggs, milk and seasonings; pour into skillet. Cook slowly. As egg mixture sets, lift slightly with a spatula to allow uncooked portion to flow underneath. Cover omelet with ½ cup Cheese, mushrooms and chives; fold in half and sprinkle with remaining Cheese. Makes 3 to 4 servings.

Wheat Germ Vegetarian Torte

The most epicurian recipes come from the healthiest people. This recipe from the label on a jar of Kretschmer® Wheat Germ is fabulous. Bake it and see.

1 cup saltine cracker crumbs (about 26 crackers)
¾ cup Kretschmer® Regular Wheat Germ, divided
8 Tbs. butter or margarine, divided
2 medium 8 ozs. zucchini, sliced
1 medium onion, sliced
1 tsp. marjoram leaves, crushed

½ tsp. salt
¼ tsp. pepper
¼ tsp. tarragon leaves, crushed
1 cup grated Monterey Jack cheese
½ cup grated Parmesan cheese
2 eggs
⅓ cup milk
1 medium tomato, thinly sliced

Combine cracker crumbs, ¼ cup wheat germ and 6 Tbs. melted butter in small bowl. Stir well. Press evenly on bottom and about 1 inch up sides of 9-inch springform pan or on bottom and sides of 9-inch pie pan. Bake at 400°F. for 8 to 10 minutes until very lightly browned. Remove from oven. Sauté zucchini and onion in remaining 2 Tbs. butter until tender-crisp. Add seasonings to vegetable mixture. Stir well. Place half the vegetables in crumb crust. Sprinkle with about 3 Tbs. of the remaining wheat germ. Top with half the cheeses, remaining vegetables, then about 3 Tbs. wheat germ. Beat eggs and milk together. Pour into center of vegetable mixture. Arrange tomato slices on top and sprinkle with remaining cheeses and wheat germ. Bake at 325°F. for 40 to 45 minutes until hot and bubbly. Makes 6 servings.

French Egg Nests

A Classic Creole recipe from Avery Island in Louisiana where Tabasco® Hot Pepper Sauce has been made for over 75 years.

2 thick slices French bread
3 Tbs. butter or margarine
2 eggs
  Salt
  Tabasco® Hot Pepper Sauce
  Grated Cheddar cheese

Take French bread slices and hollow out the center of each. Dot with butter. Break egg into each hollow. Salt lightly and add 3 drops Tabasco® Hot Pepper Sauce to each egg. Sprinkle with cheese. Bake in 325°F. oven until eggs are set. Serves 2.

Vegetable Nut Pie

When you want a hearty but meatless dish, try this vegetable nut pie. Hot from the oven it's positively superb. A smash-hit recipe ever since it first appeared in a Planters® cookbook.

1 9-inch pastry shell, unbaked
2 Tbs. Blue Bonnet® Margarine
1 cup chopped onion
½ cup chopped red bell pepper
4 cups coarsely chopped fresh spinach
¾ cup chopped Planters® Pecan Pieces or Planters® Pecan Chips
1¼ cups grated Swiss cheese
1¼ cups half-and-half
3 eggs
¾ tsp. salt
⅛ tsp. ground black pepper

Prebake pastry shell at 425°F. for 10 minutes. Melt Blue Bonnet® Margarine in a large skillet over medium heat. Add onion and red pepper; sauté until nearly tender. Stir in spinach and sauté until wilted. Sprinkle Planters® Pecan Pieces or Planters® Pecan Chips and cheese in bottom of pastry shell; spread spinach mixture over cheese layer. Beat together half-and-half, eggs, salt and pepper; pour into pie shell. Bake at 350°F. for 35 minutes, or until puffy and a knife inserted in center comes out clean. Do not overbake. Slice and serve hot. Makes 1 pie.

3.
Versatile Salads

Our American love affair with salads began out in California, as far back as the 1940's, when Gaylord Hauser, one of the first "food-for-good-health" advocates, became weight-control adviser to some of Hollywood's top box-office stars. He recommended salad, and only salad, for lunch. Greta Garbo, among others, followed his advice. In no time it seemed salad, only salad, was the most requested luncheon item at studio commissaries. Restaurants in the area vied with each other to prepare the best, most interesting salad in town, and a main-course luncheon salad was the "in" thing to serve.

These days we serve salads not just for lunch. We take them to cook-outs and tail-gate picnics. We have them for supper, feature them at parties, and make them the main attraction of the meal. In short, we love salads.

Fortunately, our food companies are just as "taken" with salads as the customer. Their test kitchens have come up with original, American salad creations from the start; and what lovely creations. Salads that bolster appetites; salads suited to be the heart of the meal; salads that are perfect to include on a buffet table, but can also stand alone as a main course; and salads that, though they seem just made for a summer day, can be served and enjoyed any time of the year.

Imagination and great taste are what our test kitchen experts have put into these recipes. They are good for you as well as great tasting and good to look at.

We lead off with three super chicken salads, each with the plus of unexpected ingredients: avocado, ripe olives, chopped apple, seedless grapes, pineapple, chopped almonds, pimientos and a tart mustard dressing.

Following these, an extra flavorful Turkey-Macaroni Salad made special with crunchy almonds and cranberry jelly cubes; a surprise hot and cold salad with Mexican flavor; a typical California creation, a perfect blend of crisp greens, shrimp, olives and cheese. And, because I know that everyone needs a bit of luxury in their lives at one time or another, a potato salad with caviar. But I haven't neglected vegetable salads either; old-fashioned corn and ever-popular bean are followed by a layered vegetable salad I know you will enjoy, plus a selection of salad dressings that are easy, inexpensive and especially good.

Once again, I assure you each recipe here is a tested success. Tested not just for accuracy, but for superb flavor. All that is needed from you are the easy putting together, the serving and the enjoyment they deserve.

Chicken Salad Habañera

Here's the chicken salad that will make everyone dance with joy. The California Olive Industry says so, and I believe it. Try it and see for yourself.

1½ cups boned, cooked chicken, in thin strips
1 cup California ripe olives, sliced in wedges
1 California avocado, cut into crescents
⅓ cup green pepper strips
¼ cup red onion, finely chopped
2 to 3 Tbs. pimiento, in thin strips
4 cups lettuce, shredded Dressing (below)

Combine ingredients; hold aside avocado. Cover and chill. Combine dressing ingredients in a jar and shake well. Refrigerate. Just before serving add avocados, shake dressing (below) and pour over salad. Toss lightly; serve on bed of shredded lettuce. Serves 4.

Dressing

⅓ cup salad oil
¼ cup red wine vinegar
¼ cup lemon juice
1 Tbs. sugar
1 tsp. salt
½ tsp. pepper
⅛ to ¼ tsp. fresh garlic, minced

New Delhi Chicken Salad

Swanson® introduced this "different from everyday" salad several years ago. It's an inspired combination of crisp apples and tender chunks of chicken punctuated by the heady flavors of Indian condiments and spices.

¼ cup mayonnaise
¼ cup sour cream
2 Tbs. finely chopped chutney
2 tsps. lemon juice
½ tsp. curry powder
¼ tsp. salt
2 5-oz. cans Swanson® Chunk Chicken

1 small apple, diced (about ½ cup)
½ cup chopped celery
2 Tbs. toasted slivered almonds
4 slices pineapple

In bowl, combine mayonnaise, sour cream, chutney, lemon juice, curry and salt. Toss lightly with Chicken, apple, celery and almonds. Chill. Serve on pineapple slices. Garnish with additional almonds if desired. Makes about 2½ cups; 4 servings.

Chicken Salad Supreme

A justly popular main-course salad that's a fine blend of ingredients with just the right amount of tangy, well-balanced dressing. A fine French chef perfected this recipe for Grey Poupon® Dijon Mustard.

¾ cup mayonnaise
3 Tbs. Grey Poupon® Dijon Mustard
2 cups cooked chicken, cubed
2 Tbs. each, chopped pimiento and pickle relish

¾ cup chopped celery
½. cup slivered toasted almonds
2 hard-cooked eggs, diced
1 Tbs. minced onion

Combine mayonnaise and mustard. Toss dressing lightly with remaining ingredients. Chill. If desired, serve on a bed of greens. Serves 4.

Heavenly Turkey Macaroni Salad

This Mueller's® brainstorm for using up that leftover roast turkey can be made a day or so ahead of time and still taste perfectly wonderful. Just toss it again shortly before serving. Serve it as a main course luncheon dish or take it in a cooler on a picnic.

8 ozs. (2 cups) Mueller's®
  Elbow Macaroni
1 cup mayonnaise
¼ cup light cream
1 cup sliced celery
1 Tbs. minced scallions
1 Tbs. minced crystallized
  ginger, if desired
1 tsp. salt

Dash pepper
2 cups diced cooked turkey
1 cup seedless grapes,
  cut in half
½ cup coarsely chopped
  walnuts
Salad greens
Jellied cranberry sauce

Cook Mueller's® Elbow Macaroni as directed on package; drain. Rinse with cold water; drain again. Meanwhile, in large salad bowl combine mayonnaise, cream, celery, scallions, ginger, salt and pepper. Add macaroni, turkey, grapes and walnuts; mix lightly. Serve on greens; garnish with cubes of cranberry sauce. May also be garnished with additional grapes and walnuts, if desired. Makes 6 servings.

Deviled Ham Stuffed Tomatoes

Though there is no end of stuffed tomato recipes here's one that's a must. It comes from the Underwood® Deviled Ham people. Use sun-ripened, fresh from the garden tomatoes and serve with hot blueberry muffins and ice tea!

2 4½-oz. cans Underwood® Deviled Ham
1 cup (4 ozs.) shredded Swiss cheese
½ cup chopped pimiento-stuffed olives
2 Tbs. chopped onion
4 medium tomatoes, cut into quarters, to within ¼ inch of bottom

In a bowl, mix together deviled ham, cheese, olives and onion. Spoon mixture into center of tomatoes. Chill. Makes 4 servings.

Celebration Salad

The seasoning in this salad is superb; the recipe is from a Mueller's® Elbow Macaroni package and is one of the best ever.

Cooked asparagus spears
Bottled Italian dressing
8 ozs. (2 cups) Mueller's® Elbow Macaroni
¾ cup mayonnaise
2 Tbs. catsup
½ tsp. prepared horseradish
¼ tsp. dry mustard
2 Tbs. sliced scallions
2 cups slivered cooked ham
1 cup sliced celery
Watercress
Cherry tomatoes

Marinate asparagus in Italian dressing overnight, or at least 3 to 4 hours. Cook Mueller's® Elbow Macaroni as directed on package; drain. Rinse with cold water; drain again. In bowl blend mayonnaise, catsup, horseradish, mustard and scallions; toss in macaroni, ham and celery. To serve, arrange asparagus spears on platter; top with macaroni salad. Garnish with watercress and cherry tomatoes. Makes 6 servings.

Salad Oscar

The contrast of piping hot sausages and dressing on cold lettuce and vegetables sparked with crisp croutons is positively sensational. Just do serve right away or the lettuce will wilt. A plus-extra good recipe from the plus-extra good cooks at Oscar Mayer®.

1 12-oz. package Oscar Mayer® Cheese Smokies (links)
1 small head lettuce, (about 1 lb.)
½ medium green pepper, sliced into rings
2 slices onion, separated into rings
1 medium tomato, cut into wedges
¼ cup sliced fresh mushrooms, cauliflowerettes or ripe olives
¾ cup creamy French dressing
½ cup flavored croutons

Cut links into ½-inch slices; set aside. Wash lettuce; use darker green leaves to line individual serving plates. Tear remaining lettuce into bite-size pieces. Arrange lettuce pieces and remaining vegetables on lettuce-lined plates. In saucepan combine smoked sausage links with French dressing; heat to boiling, stirring often. Reduce heat to low; cover; heat 5 minutes. Top salad with smoked sausage link mixture and croutons. Serve immediately. Makes 2 to 4 servings.

California Tossed Salad

Beautiful, just beautiful, is what I call this salad. First served many years ago in the executive restaurant at MGM Studios in Hollywood, it was adapted for a national ad by the Diamond® Walnut Company.

½ cup large pieces
   Diamond® Walnuts
⅓ cup salad oil
1 tsp. seasoned salt
3 Tbs. lemon juice
1 tsp. granulated sugar
¼ tsp. marjoram, crumbled
¼ tsp. dill weed
1½ quarts torn mixed salad
   greens

6 ozs. cooked shrimp or
   prawns (or 1 5-oz. can
   drained)
1 large tomato, cut in
   wedges
¼ cup radish slices
¼ cup ripe olive slices
2 Tbsp. chopped chives or
   green onion
¼ cup cheese cubes

Toast walnuts lightly in small skillet over low heat with 1 tsp. oil, stirring frequently, about 5 minutes. Remove from heat; sprinkle with ¼ tsp. seasoned salt. Cool. Beat together remaining oil, salt, lemon juice, sugar, marjoram and dill weed. In large bowl, combine greens, shrimp, tomato, radish, olives and chives. Stir dressing; pour over salad. Toss until evenly coated. Add walnuts; toss again. Sprinkle with cheese. Serve at once. Makes 2 quarts salad, 4 large servings.

Crescent City Salad

Gulf shrimp and "creole" tomato chunks in a caraway-flavored dressing are featured in this New Orleans–style salad from Heinz®.

⅔ cup salad oil
⅓ cup Heinz® Wine Vinegar
2 Tbs. chopped parsley
1 clove garlic, minced
½ tsp. caraway seeds
½ tsp. salt
½ lb. fresh mushrooms, sliced

6 cups torn salad greens, chilled
½ lb. cooked shrimp
1 cup tomato chunks
½ cup chopped onion

Combine first 6 ingredients in jar. Cover; shake vigorously. Add mushrooms; chill to blend flavors. Shake again before tossing with salad greens, shrimp, tomatoes and onion. Makes 8 servings (about 8 cups).

Cold Salmon & Cucumber Salad

A delicious new way to turn canned salmon into a spectacular cold main-course entrée. It's from the Dannon® Yogurt advertising pages.

2 envelopes unflavored gelatin
1½ cups chicken broth
½ cup mayonnaise
2 Tbs. lemon juice
2 cups Dannon® Plain Yogurt
2 Tbs. minced onion

2 Tbs. chopped dill
1 1-lb. can salmon, drained with skin and bones removed
2 cucumbers peeled, chopped and seeds removed
Salt to taste

Stir gelatin and chicken broth over low heat until gelatin is dissolved. Beat in mayonnaise and lemon juice. Chill until the mixture is thick and syrupy. Fold in yogurt, dill, onion, cucumbers and salmon. Pour into mold. Chill until set. Unmold, garnish with hard-boiled eggs, parsley, tomatoes and put on a bed of cooked rice or lettuce. Serves 4 to 6.

Ivan's Potato Salad

I found this recipe over 10 years ago in a folder that came in a box holding a jar of Romanoff® Icelandic Lumpfish Caviar. It's a sensational salad, not nearly as expensive as it looks and positively delicious. You'll be asked for the recipe, I guarantee it, every time it's served.

10 medium potatoes,
  peeled and thinly sliced
  (6 cups)
 6 Tbs. oil
 3 Tbs. vinegar
 3 Tbs. lemon juice
 ¼ cup chopped onion
 ¼ tsp. powdered dill

Dash of salt and pepper
 4 hard-cooked eggs,
  chopped
 ¼ cup mayonnaise
 3 Tbs. (½ oz.) Romanoff®
  Caviar
  Additional Caviar for
  garnish

Cook potatoes in boiling salted water until barely tender, about eight minutes. Drain. In large bowl, combine oil, vinegar, lemon juice, onion, dill, salt and pepper. Add potatoes; toss to coat. Mash eggs with mayonnaise. Gently stir in Caviar and fold into potatoes. Cover; keep cold. At serving time, garnish with additional Caviar. Makes 8 generous servings.

Mexican Macaroni Salad

A hearty meatless main-course salad high in protein; a favorite luncheon special at the Hellmann's® and Best Foods® Executive Dining Room.

 1 cup Hellmann's® Best
  Foods® Real Mayonnaise
 ⅓ cup skim milk
 2 tsps. instant chopped
  onion
 1 tsp. salt
 1 tsp. chili powder
 ⅛ tsp. garlic powder

 6 drops hot pepper sauce
 1 8-oz. package elbow
  macaroni, cooked,
  drained
 1 16-oz. can red kidney
  beans, well drained
 1 cup diced part-skim
  Mozzarella cheese (4 ozs.)

In large bowl stir together first 7 ingredients. Add remaining ingredients; toss to coat well. Cover; chill at least 2 hours. Makes 8 1-cup servings.

Southwestern Noodle Salad

An unusual approach to the traditional macaroni salad from the test kitchens of the French® Company. Make it two or three days ahead, but do taste before serving since it may need a dash more salt and an extra splash of vinegar.

1 lb. medium to small shell macaroni, cooked al dente, thoroughly drained
⅔ cup cider vinegar
¼ cup vegetable oil
1 cup minced celery (about 2 stalks)
½ cup chopped (about ½ large) green pepper
6 green onions, minced
1 2-oz. jar chopped pimiento, drained
3 generous dashes French® Company Worcestershire sauce

3 dashes hot pepper sauce
1 Tbs. minced, roasted green chili pepper
1 tsp. salt
½ tsp. freshly ground pepper
1 15-oz. can black-eyed peas, drained
1 12-oz. can corn, drained
½ cup pitted black olives, drained and chopped
1 2-oz. jar green olives with pimiento, drained and chopped
⅓ cup mayonnaise (about)

Place macaroni in large bowl. Pour vinegar over and let stand while preparing other ingredients. Add all other ingredients to macaroni and mix well. Cover and refrigerate 2 to 3 days. Taste for seasoning before serving. Makes 12 servings.

Four-Layer Vegetable Salad

One of the best salad ideas ever from Land O Lakes®. You make the dressing in the salad bowl, layer on the salad and refrigerate until ready to toss and serve. Super easy, super good.

Dressing

½ cup Land O Lakes® Sour Cream

½ cup salad dressing or mayonnaise

1 Tbs. prepared mustard

½ tsp. dill weed

Salad

¼ cup chopped green onion

¼ cup chopped celery

¼ cup chopped green pepper

1 cup frozen peas, thawed and drained

5 cups torn head lettuce (½ to ¾ head)

1 cup (4 ozs.) shredded Land O Lakes® Medium Natural Cheddar Cheese

5 slices bacon, fried and finely crumbled

Combine all dressing ingredients in large bowl; blend well. Layer onion, celery, green pepper, peas and lettuce over dressing. Sprinkle with Cheese and top with bacon. Cover and refrigerate overnight or at least 4 hours. Toss before serving. Makes 6 1-cup servings.

Tangy Bean Salad

An ever-popular historic curiosity, this is the first of many versions of Three-Bean Salad and a Stokely–Van Camp® original.

½ cup white vinegar
½ cup sugar
½ cup vegetable oil
½ cup chopped onion
½ cup chopped green
   pepper
1 16-oz. can Stokely's®
   Finest Cut Green Beans,
   drained

1 15½-oz. can Stokely's®
   Finest Cut Wax Beans,
   drained
1 15-oz. can Stokely's®
   Finest Dark Red Kidney
   Beans, drained
Red onion rings (optional)

Combine vinegar, sugar, oil, onion, and green pepper in large bowl and mix well. Drain all Beans and add to dressing. Toss gently and marinate in refrigerator for at least 4 hours or overnight. Serve in bowl lined with lettuce. May be garnished with onion rings. Makes 10 servings.

Cool Corn Salad

The perfect picnic salad developed by Stokely–Van Camp® cooks back when they first introduced canned whole kernel corn. It's a recipe people have asked for ever since that time.

¼ cup commercial sour
   cream
¼ cup mayonnaise
1 Tbs. prepared mustard
2 tsps. white vinegar
1 tsp. sugar
¼ tsp. salt
⅛ tsp. pepper

1 17-oz. can Stokely's®
   Finest Whole Kernel
   Golden Corn, drained
1 2-oz. jar Stokely's® Finest
   Sliced Pimientos, drained
   and diced
2 carrots, peeled and grated
½ cup diced onion

In medium-size bowl, make dressing by combining sour cream, mayonnaise, mustard, vinegar, sugar, salt, and pepper. Add remaining ingredients and toss to blend. Cover and refrigerate at least 1 hour. Makes 4 to 6 servings.

Studio City Special

Remember carrot-raisin salad? Here it is, made elegant by Sun-Maid®, the raisin people.

2 cups grated carrot (4 large carrots)
½ cup Sun-Maid® Seedless Raisins
1 13 ¼-oz. can pineapple tidbits, drained

½ cup mayonnaise
1 Tbs. instant minced onion
1 tsp. prepared mustard
⅛ tsp. salt
½ tsp. celery seed

Pare and cut carrots into chunks. Whirl (dry) in blender until grated. Combine all ingredients. Serve in lettuce cups. Makes 4 servings.

Tart Cranberry Mold

This just might be the recipe you've been trying to track down. It's that tart-sweet cranberry mold your mother or perhaps her best friend always served with the Thanksgiving turkey. There are dozens of variations, but this one from Heinz® is, in my opinion, the best. Certainly it's one of the first and appeared in a booklet printed back in 1946.

1 3-oz package lemon-flavored gelatin
1½ cups boiling water
1½ cups raw cranberries
½ medium orange, seeded, unpeeled

⅓ cup chopped Heinz® Sweet Pickles
3 Tbs. sugar
2 cups prepared whipped-topping mix

Dissolve gelatin in boiling water; chill until slightly thickened. Meanwhile, put cranberries and orange through food chopper using fine blade. Stir in pickles and sugar. Fold cranberry mixture into thickened gelatin; then gently fold in whipped-topping mix. Pour into a 1-quart (or 8½-cup) molds. Chill until firm. Unmold on lettuce or endive. Makes 8 servings.

California Salad Dressing

This easy to prepare homemade salad dressing has been a favorite for years in The R. T. French® Company consumer services kitchens.

1 envelope French's® Sour
   Cream Sauce Mix
½ cup milk
1 cup mayonnaise
2 Tbs. French's® Parsley
   Flakes

2 Tbs. vinegar
2 Tbs. anchovy paste, if
   desired
½ tsp. French's® Garlic Salt
⅛ tsp. French's® Pepper
   Salad greens

Prepare Sour Cream Sauce with milk as directed on envelope. Stir in mayonnaise, Parsley Flakes, vinegar, anchovy paste, Garlic Salt and Pepper. Serve with salad greens. Makes 2 cups dressing.

Note: If preferred, toss salad with crisp croutons and tiny cooked shrimp just before adding dressing.

Yogurt "Mayonnaise"

Requests for this recipe have been pouring in ever since it was developed at The Dannon® test kitchens in the 1960's.

1 cup Dannon® Plain Yogurt
2 Tbs. butter
4 Tbs. flour
1 cup milk

1 egg yolk
2 Tbs. lemon juice
½ tsp. dry mustard
½ tsp. salt

Melt the butter in a skillet and stir in flour. Add milk all at once and stir over medium heat until thick. Remove from heat and beat in egg yolk, lemon juice, mustard and salt. Stir in yogurt and cool. Makes approximately 2 cups.

Cucumber Parsley Dressing

A delicious idea for green salads or cold fish; a Hollywood favorite back in the 1930's adapted by the Dannon® Yogurt people.

½ cup mayonnaise
1 cup peeled, seeded and chopped cucumber
1 cup chopped parsley
1 clove garlic, minced
½ tsp. salt
⅛ tsp. ground black pepper
1 cup Dannon® Plain Yogurt

Stir together first 6 ingredients. Stir in Dannon® Yogurt. Chill. Makes about 2 cups.

HELLMANN'S BEST DRESSINGS
- -

Hellmann's® and Best Foods Mayonnaise has developed literally hundreds of great salad dressings over the past thirty years. Here are three of the most requested—top favorites all.

Remoulade Dressing

1 cup Hellmann's® Best Foods Real Mayonnaise
4 sprigs parsley
2 Tbs. chili sauce
2 Tbs. capers
2 Tbs. milk
2 tsps. prepared mustard
1 small clove garlic

Place ingredients in blender container; cover. Blend until smooth. Cover; chill. Makes 1¼ cups.

Russian Dressing

1 cup Hellmann's® Best Foods Real
   Mayonnaise
⅓ cup chili sauce or catsup
2 tsps. lemon juice
1½ tsps. sugar

Stir ingredients together. Cover; chill. Makes 1⅓ cups.

Thousand Island Dressing

1 cup Hellmann's® Best Foods Real Mayonnaise
⅓ cup chili sauce or catsup
3 Tbs. sweet pickle relish
1 hard-cooked egg, chopped

Stir ingredients together. Cover; chill. Makes 1½ cups.

Tangy Coconut Salad Dressing
for Fruit, Ham
or Chicken Salads

**The Holland House® Cream of Coconut label says this lovely
and different salad dressing is equally good on fresh fruit
salad or on a salad of ham or chicken. I can't decide which I
like best.**

½ cup corn oil
½ cup Coco Casa® Cream of
   Coconut
1 6-oz. can frozen
   concentrated orange
   juice, thawed and
   undiluted

¼ tsp. curry powder
½ tsp. salt

In a bowl, combine all ingredients and beat until smooth and thick. Chill until ready to serve. Beat again and toss with salad when ready to serve. Makes 1¾ cups.

Honey Dressing

The good cooks at Kraft® suggest this creamy-smooth dressing for fruit salad.

¾ cup Kraft® Real Mayonnaise
⅓ cup honey
1 Tbs. grated lemon rind
¾ tsp. lemon juice
¼ tsp. ginger

Combine Mayonnaise, honey, lemon rind, lemon juice and ginger; mix well. Chill. Makes 1 cup.

4.

Soups to Make the Pot Smile

"It's a day to make the pot smile," my mother used to say, and it was; a cold, frosty day in late fall or deep into winter; a perfect day for the slowly simmered, rich and hearty soup she liked to prepare. Such soups do have a way of stirring you to life but the idea that all good soup must take hours to prepare can be laid to rest right here and now. Soup need not always be a day-long project. Here are quick-cooking soups to make, not just the pot, but you and your family smile with satisfaction from first spoonful to last.

A good soup can make the meal. In fact, with some homemade bread and a salad or some fresh fruit and cheese for dessert it can be the meal, one of the finest you can possibly prepare. Just try Frank Morgan's Pirate Bean Soup (page 125) with thin slices of lightly buttered Russian Black Bread (page 155) or the Italian Pasta Pot (page 123) with freshly baked Pita Bread (page 160) and you'll see what I mean.

On the other hand there are a great many types of soup—delicate as well as hearty—and they all have their place. Nothing pleases me so much as a fine China cup filled with classic Purée Mongole at the start of an elegant dinner. I think Spanish Bisque the all-time perfect soup for a summer lucheon, and when it comes to singing out the old, kissing in the new, nothing, but nothing, will take the place of a great New Year's Eve oyster stew—the perfect soup to serve with champagne.

You'll find these all here and quite a few more. The nice thing is that whatever you make you can be sure of success. Each recipe has been tested and retested so that you can relax and enjoy both the making and serving as well as the eating.

Danish Tomato Soup

Ungarnished hot consommé looks so forlorn, and plain to-mato soup, no matter if it is red, ought to have a little some-thing to dress it up. It does with this elegant version from the Blue Diamond® Almond Growers.

1 10½-oz. can condensed tomato soup
1 can milk
⅛ tsp. dill weed
   Sour cream and toasted blanched slivered
   almonds for garnish

Combine and heat ingredients through. To serve, gar-nish with a dollop of dairy sour cream and plenty of toasted blanched slivered almonds. Makes 3 servings.

Easy French Onion Soup

If this easy onion soup recipe and its deluxe variation from *Bon Appetit* magazine aren't in your file, they should be. Here they are if you missed them; French's® Worcestershire Sauce creations and among the best of their kind.

2 Tbs. butter or margarine
1 large onion, sliced
½ tsp. sugar
1 10½-oz. can beef bouillon
1¼ cups water
2 Tbs. French's®
   Worcestershire Sauce

Melt butter in medium-size saucepan. Add onion and sugar; cook and stir 5 to 10 minutes until lightly browned. Add bouillon, water and Worcestershire Sauce; simmer 10 to 15 minutes.

Deluxe French Onion Soup

4 slices French or pumpernickel bread
   Easy French Onion Soup
   (above)
½ cup Swiss cheese, shredded
1 Tbs. Parmesan cheese, grated

Arrange bread on baking sheet; bake in 300°F. oven 20 to 30 minutes, until crisp and dry. Spoon soup into 4 oven-proof serving dishes; top each with 1 slice bread and sprinkle generously with cheese mixture. Place under broiler 2 to 3 minutes to melt cheese. For soup bowls which are not oven-proof, toast bread as directed. Add cheese and broil, then place on hot soup. Makes 4 servings.

Spanish Bisque

First served at the elegant Beverly Wilshire Hotel in Beverly Hills, California. An exclusive recipe that was *not* available until someone wrote the Avocado Advisory Board who then sent a home economist from their test kitchen to taste, and duplicate the special soup. It was well worth the trip!

2 avocados	Dash cayenne
1⅔ cups (13¾-oz. can)	Dash garlic powder
chicken broth	1 cup light cream
3 Tbs. lemon juice	Garniture (below)
¾ tsp. salt	

Puree avocados with broth, lemon juice and seasonings. Blend in cream; cover and chill. Serve with your choice of the garnishes below. Makes 6 to 8 servings.

Garnishes: Crumbled crisp bacon, chopped toasted almonds, buttered croutons, chili relish (mix 2 Tbs. minced onion with 2 canned green chili peppers, chopped, and 3 canned pimientos, chopped), diced ham, slivered prosciutto, finely chopped hard-cooked egg or chopped anchovy fillets.

Gazpacho Soup

A "where-did-you-get-the-recipe?" soup. Some cooks won't tell, but this really great, smash-hit gazpacho recipe can be found on the label of a Snap-E-Tom® Bloody Thomas Mix can.

1 10-oz. can Snap-E-Tom® Tomato Cocktail (or 2 6-oz. cans)
½ medium cucumber, chopped
1 medium tomato, chopped
1 Tbs. sugar
¼ cup red wine vinegar
¼ cup salad oil

2 10-oz. cans Snap-E-Tom® Tomato Cocktail (or 3 6-oz. cans)
1 medium tomato, finely chopped
½ medium cucumber, finely chopped
1 small onion, finely chopped

Blend together in blender the first 6 ingredients. Add these to the last 4 ingredients and chill. Serve very cold with at least 2 of the following garnishes: croutons, chopped hard-boiled egg whites, chopped green bell pepper, chopped fresh onion. Makes 6 servings.

Spicy Jellied Consommé

On the subject of chilled soups, this one gives a different twist to your taste buds. It's those few drops of Angostura® that add the subtle, exotic flavor.

2 Tbs. minced chives
¾ tsp. Angostura®
1 can consommé

Add chives and Angostura® to each can of consommé. Chill until jelled, beat slightly with fork. Serve in cups.

Leek and Potato Soup

**You'll find this recipe on the back of a package of Frieda's®
Finest Leeks. It's in the produce department and yes, there is
a Frieda. She's a versatile and talented woman who runs her
own business and is a great cook besides. This is her own
recipe for vichyssoise, or Leek and Potato soup if you prefer.**

4 leeks, white parts only
3 Tbs. butter
3 potatoes
1 tsp. salt
1 quart chicken stock

1½ pints rich milk
1 pint heavy cream
   (half-and-half)
   Chopped chives

Slice leeks thinly; peel and slice potatoes. Cook leeks in butter until limp. Transfer them to the soup pot and add the potatoes. Add salt and broth; let simmer until potatoes are very tender. Put contents of pot through a sieve; return mixture to soup pot and add milk. Let simmer a few minutes. Correct seasoning and add a little ground white pepper if you like. Chill in the refrigerator. Just before serving, beat in the cream. Serve in chilled bowls and sprinkle the top with chopped chives. Serves 6.

Potage Senegalese

From *Campbell's® Best Recipes* cookbook. In my opinion it's very good served hot, but positively fabulous when well chilled, then ladled into icy-cold bowls.

1 10¾-oz. can Campbell's Condensed Cream of Chicken Soup
1 soup can water
½ cup light cream
¼ cup applesauce

2 Tbs. shredded coconut
1 tsp. curry powder
½ tsp. garlic salt
½ tsp. onion powder
1 avocado, sliced

In saucepan, combine all ingredients except avocado. Heat; stir occasionally. Top each serving with avocado. Makes about 3½ cups.

For chilled soup: Prepare recipe as above; chill 6 hours. Serve in chilled bowls.

Corn Chowder

They tell me at Stokely–Van Camp® this chowder is their "best ever" for a cold winter's day.

3 Tbs. butter or margarine
1 cup diced cooked ham
½ cup chopped onion
½ cup shopped celery
½ cup chopped green or red pepper
2 cups chicken broth
1 cup diced potatoes
⅛ tsp. pepper

1½ cups milk
½ cup heavy cream
1 17-oz. can Stokely's Finest® Whole Kernel Golden Corn
1 2-oz. jar Stokely's Finest® Sliced Pimientos, drained
Paprika

Melt butter in large saucepan. Sauté ham 5 minutes and set aside. Sauté onion, celery and green pepper until onion is transparent. Add chicken broth, potatoes, and pepper. Cover and cook over moderate heat about 20 minutes, or until potatoes are just tender. Add milk, cream, corn, reserved ham and pimientos. Reduce heat and cook until thoroughly heated. Do not boil. Spoon into bowls and garnish each serving with paprika. Makes 6 servings.

Golden Cheese Soup

This is what I call a light-hearty soup—light, but with hearty flavor. It's a Land O Lakes® recipe from their Process American Cheese package. A "just right" soup for a chilly night.

¼ cup Land O Lakes® Sweet Cream Butter
½ cup shredded carrot
⅓ cup all-purpose flour
1 Tbs. instant minced onion or 3 Tbs. fresh chopped onion
1 tsp. instant chicken bouillon
¼ tsp. salt

¼ tsp. dry mustard
¼ tsp. curry powder, if desired
⅛ tsp. pepper
3 cups milk
¼ tsp. hot pepper sauce
2 cups (8 ozs.) shredded Land O Lakes® Process American Cheese
½ cup beer

In heavy 2-quart saucepan melt butter over medium heat. Sauté carrots in melted butter until tender (5 to 7 minutes). Remove from heat; stir in flour, onion, bouillon and seasonings until well combined. Slowly stir in milk and hot pepper sauce until smooth. Return to heat. Add cheese. Cook over medium heat, stirring frequently, until mixture thickens and comes to a boil. Boil gently for 1 minute, stirring constantly. Reduce heat; add beer and heat through. Serve immediately. Garnish with popcorn. Makes 4 servings.

Tip: If using fresh onion, sauté with carrot until tender. To reheat or thin soup, add more beer or milk.

Purée Mongole

This elegant classic was developed at the Campbell's® Soup test kitchen way back, even before your mother's time, but it's still very much in fashion.

1 11¼-oz. can Campbell's®
Condensed Green Pea
Soup
1 10¾-oz. can Campbell's®
Condensed Tomato Soup
1 cup milk
1 cup water
Dash curry powder, optional

In saucepan, stir Green Pea Soup until smooth; gradually blend in remaining ingredients. Heat; stir occasionally. Do not boil. Makes about 4½ cups.

Oyster Bisque

Oyster Bisque has always been a New Year's Eve tradition at our house, but no one was ever quite as satisfied as with the results I obtained from this recipe about 10 years ago from the Tabasco® Hot Pepper Sauce people.

1 dozen (1 pint) shucked
large raw oysters
1 cup oyster liquor
3 cups milk
1 cup heavy cream
1 slice onion
2 stalks celery
1 sprig parsley
1 bay leaf
⅓ cup butter or margarine,
melted
⅓ cup flour
1¾ tsps. salt
½ tsp. Tabasco® Hot Pepper
Sauce
Chopped chives

Drain oysters; reserve 1 cup liquor. Dice oysters into saucepan and add liquor; slowly bring oysters to boiling point; remove. In same saucepan scald milk and cream with onion, celery, parsley and bay leaf; strain. Blend butter with flour, salt and Tabasco® Hot Pepper Sauce. Slowly stir in scalded milk; stir over low heat until thickened. Add oysters and cooking liquid; heat to serving temperature. Garnish with chopped chives. Makes 6 to 8 servings.

Seafood Bisque

A new idea whose time has come; a delicious "quickly" soup from Birds-Eye® destined to become a cross-country favorite.

1 8-oz. package Birds-Eye® Green Peas with
  Cream Sauce
1 cup milk
1 cup half-and-half
1 7¾-oz. can red salmon, flaked*
1 Tbs. catsup

Combine vegetable, milk and half-and-half in saucepan. Bring to a full boil over medium-high heat, stirring occasionally. Remove from heat and stir until sauce is smooth. Add salmon and catsup. Cover; simmer 5 minutes. Makes 3 servings.

* Or use 1 7-oz. can tuna, drained and flaked

Seafood Gumbo

After much debate, this is one of the ten soup recipes rated highest in favor at the Hunt-Wesson® test kitchen.

1 clove garlic, minced
1 large onion, chopped
½ green pepper, diced
¼ cup pure vegetable oil
1 14½-oz. can Hunt's® Whole Tomatoes
1 6-oz. can Hunt's® Tomato Paste
3 cups water
1 Tbs. Worcestershire sauce
2 tsp. salt

1 bay leaf
½ tsp. chili powder
½ tsp. crushed basil leaves
½ lb. crab meat
½ lb. raw shrimp, shelled and cleaned
½ lb. fresh haddock or halibut, cut in chunks
1 10-oz. pkg. frozen sliced okra, partially thawed
3 cups hot cooked rice

In a Dutch oven, sauté garlic, onion and green pepper in oil, stirring until tender. Add remaining ingredients except seafood, okra and rice. Simmer, uncovered, 45 minutes; remove bay leaf. Add crab, shrimp, haddock and okra; cover and simmer 10 to 12 minutes. Serve in soup bowls over rice. Makes 8 servings.

Italian Pasta Pot

Viva La Roma! **Trust Campbell's®, the soup people, to top even themselves. Serve an Italian antipasto, some crusty bread, red wine, then fresh fruit and cheese for dessert. Your supper party will be the talk of the crowd.**

½ cup chopped green pepper
1 large clove garlic, minced
¼ tsp. rosemary leaves, crushed
2 Tbs. olive oil
3 10¾-oz. cans Campbell's® Tomato Soup

3 soup cans water
1 about 16-oz can chick peas, drained
1 cup cooked small shell macaroni
2 tsps. chopped anchovy fillets

In large saucepan, cook pepper with garlic and rosemary in oil until tender. Stir in soup and water. Add remaining ingredients. Heat; stir occasionally. Garnish with grated Parmesan cheese, if desired. Makes about 9½ cups, 6 to 8 servings.

Zuppa Pasta Fagiola

This recipe, from Mueller's,® makes a lot of soup. If there are only two or three of you, make it all up to the point of adding the pasta. Freeze half and add ½ cup pasta to the remainder and continue to cook until tender. And there you have it, two superb supper soups. Served with good bread and cheese, each portion is a meal in itself.

¾ pound dried white kidney or lima beans	¼ tsp. rubbed sage
Water	¼ tsp. thyme leaves
Ham shank (about 2 lbs) or ham bone	6 cups water
2 cloves garlic, minced	¼ cup olive oil
4 medium firm tomatoes, peeled and chopped	1 cup dry white wine
½ tsp. pepper	1 tsp. salt
	¼ tsp. pepper
	2 ozs. (1 cup) Mueller's® Twist Macaroni

Soak beans in water overnight; drain. Remove skin and excess fat from ham shank. In large kettle combine beans, ham shank, garlic, 2 of the chopped tomatoes, ½ tsp. pepper, sage, thyme and 6 cups of water. Bring to a boil; cover and simmer gently 2 hours, or until beans are tender. Remove shank from kettle; dice meat and return to kettle. While beans are cooking, combine olive oil, the remaining 2 chopped tomatoes, wine, salt and ¼ tsp. pepper in medium saucepan. Simmer, uncovered, 20 minutes. Pour into bean mixture. Bring to a boil; add

Macaroni and continue to cook 9 to 12 minutes or until macaroni is tender. Serve in large soup bowls. 8 to 10 servings.

Pirate Bean Soup

Actor Frank Morgan (remember him as the wizard in the *Wizard of Oz*?) developed this recipe for his brother Ralph's import business. It soon became a favorite with his show biz pals whose children and childrens' children wrote Angostura® asking if they could possibly obtain the original recipe. Indeed they can. It's in this company's permanent file of "all-time best."

2½ cups dried pea beans
  1 onion, sliced
  1 tsp. bacon fat
  1 tsp. salt
  ⅛ tsp. pepper
  ½ cup catsup
  1 Tbs. Angostura®

Wash beans thoroughly, cover with cold water and soak overnight. Add water to make about 4 cups and simmer for one hour. Sauté onion in bacon fat until golden. Add onion, salt and pepper to beans and continue simmering for another two hours. Just before removing from fire, add catsup and Angostura®, and stir well. Makes 6 servings.

Frankfurter Creole Chowder

Considered one of the best of the best-tasting "budget-minded" soups at Campbell's®.

1 lb. frankfurters, cut in ½-inch slices
¼ tsp. basil or thyme leaves, crushed
2 Tbs. butter or margarine
1 11½-oz. can Campbell's® Condensed Split Pea with Ham Soup
1 10¾-oz. can Campbell's® Condensed Cream of Potato Soup
½ soup can water
1 can (about 8 ozs.) tomatoes, cut up
1 can (about 8 ozs.) whole kernel corn, undrained

In large saucepan, brown frankfurters with basil in butter. Add soups; gradually stir in water. Add remaining ingredients. Heat; stir occasionally. Makes about 6 cups.

5.

Side Dishes

The complaint I've heard most often in a lifetime of cooking, eating and talking about food is, "Well, the meat (or chicken or fish) was good, but the side dishes were dull." Too often this was true. We have all experienced the downright boredom of unadorned, steamed vegetables; bland, flavorless, overcooked rice; and plain-jane, foil-wrapped, baked potatoes, lackluster green beans, tasteless beets and coarse broccoli, unseasoned and ungarnished.

Such side dishes are worse than dull, they are horrible, and any cook who serves them should be made to eat nothing else. When I hear parents saying "Little Lucy won't eat potatoes," or, "The children just don't like vegetables," I wonder what the poor child is being offered. Certainly not the vegetables or potatoes you'll find here.

The trick to preparing side dishes that everyone, including the children, will eat and enjoy is to put the same creativity and just plain good cooking into the meal. That's just what was done with the recipes that follow. Interesting and truly delicious, quick and easy to prepare, each one can insure your reputation as a cook who never, but never, serves a dull meal. Just try these combinations; broiled ground lamb patties and Grecian Rice, with chopped almonds and raisins, (page 132); baked ham and Sweet Potatoes with Cashews (page 134); roast chicken with Old Fashioned Corn Pudding and Confetti Green Beans (pages 136–137); baked fish fillets with Lemony Vegetable Sauté (page 138). But that's just a few. In this chapter I have gathered together a collection of old favorites from our test-kitchen experts. I tried them all and as I did, I found each one was better than the last. Each is a triumph of flavor, a great addition to any cook's collection, and a grand way to add extra sparkle, not to mention vitamins and minerals, at low cost, to every meal that you serve.

Charleston Perloo
with Mushrooms

What's the difference between Pilafs, Pilaus and Perloos? Down in Texas at the Uncle Ben's® Rice test kitchens they say there's no basic difference; a classic Pilaf, which calls for sautéing the rice and simmering in broth with regionally favorite foods and seasonings, is known by a variety of names in different countries. This very popular one was developed about 10 years ago from an old Charleston, South Carolina, recipe.

½ pound fresh
   mushrooms, sliced
1 clove garlic
1 Tbs. olive or vegetable oil
2 Tbs. butter or margarine
1 cup thinly sliced onion
1 cup Uncle Ben's®
   Converted Brand Rice

2¼ cups chicken broth
¼ cup dry white wine
1½ tsps. salt
¼ tsp. white pepper
¼ cup freshly grated
   Parmesan cheese
2 Tbs. chopped parsley

Sauté mushrooms and garlic in olive oil in 10-inch skillet until mushrooms are tender, but not brown. Remove and reserve mushrooms; discard garlic. Add butter to skillet. Sauté onion until tender. Add rice; cook, stirring constantly, 5 minutes. Add chicken broth, mushrooms, wine, salt and pepper. Bring to boil; reduce heat. Cover tightly and simmer 20 minutes. Remove from heat. Stir in cheese and parsley. Let stand, covered, until all liquid is absorbed, about 5 minutes. Makes 6 servings.

Rice à L'Orange

**Here's a simple, but sensational recipe idea from Sunkist®
Growers.**

3 to 4 cups hot cooked rice
1 tsp. fresh grated orange
 peel
1 Sunkist® navel orange,
 peeled and cut in bite-
 size pieces

¼ cup chopped nuts, sliced
 green onions, sliced ripe
 olives or toasted sesame
 seed

To the rice, stir in orange peel and Sunkist® Orange and
then add one of the last ingredients for extra flavor.

Orange Rice

**Rice becomes party fare when done as is this pilaf from the
Angostura® Bitters test kitchens.**

1 6-oz. can frozen orange
 juice
2½ cups water
 ¼ tsp. ground saffron

1 Tbs. Angostura®
2 Tbs. butter
3 cups precooked rice

In a 2-quart saucepan mix orange juice with water, saffron, Angostura® and butter. Bring to a boil. Slowly stir in
rice. Stir to blend well. Remove from heat, cover, and let
stand for 10 minutes. Stir with a fork to fluff. Makes 8
servings.

Grecian Rice

**Just about every would-be good cook who tasted this recipe
wanted to serve it. The Blue Diamond® Almond Company**

used it in a booklet, but before that it appeared in national advertisements.

3 Tbs. butter or margarine
½ cup finely chopped onion
½ cup finely chopped green pepper
2 cloves garlic, minced or pressed
1 cup long grain rice

2 cups beef bouillon
1 tsp. cinnamon
½ tsp. salt
⅔ cup Blue Diamond® Chopped Natural Almonds
½ cup dark, seedless raisins

In large skillet melt butter; sauté onion, green pepper and garlic until barely tender. Add rice and cook, stirring often, until lightly toasted, about 4 to 6 minutes. Stir in bouillon, cinnamon and salt; cover and simmer 10 minutes. Stir in almonds and raisins; continue cooking, covered, another 5 minutes or until all liquid is absorbed. Makes 4 servings.

Guacamole Potatoes

The California avocado people ran this recipe in an ad a few years ago and it's been in my own permanent file ever since. I include it here because it's one of the best of the best of baked stuffed potatoes.

4 baking potatoes
1 California avocado
2 Tbs. sour cream
  Dash salt and pepper
4 slices bacon, crisply cooked and crumbled

Scrub potatoes and rub skins with shortening. Prick skins with fork to allow steam to escape; bake in 375°F. oven for 1¼ to 1½ hours. Mash avocado with fork to chunky texture and mix in sour cream and seasonings. When potatoes are done, cut down the center, spoon in avocado mixture and sprinkle on crumbled bacon.

Saucy Skillet Potatoes

A positively inspired way to prepare potatoes for company from the Hellmann's® and Best Foods® Real Mayonnaise people. Everything but the final heating can be done ahead.

1 Tbs. margarine	¼ tsp. pepper
1 cup chopped onions	4 medium potatoes,
½ cup Hellmann's® Best	cooked, peeled, sliced
Foods® Real Mayon-	(4 cups)
naise	1 Tbs. chopped parsley
⅓ cup cider vinegar	1 Tbs. cooked crumbled
1 Tbs. sugar	bacon
1¾ tsps. salt	

In large skillet melt margarine over medium heat. Add onions; cook 2 to 3 minutes or until tender-crisp. Stir in next 5 ingredients. Add potatoes; cook, stirring constantly, 2 minutes or until hot (do not boil). Garnish with parsley and bacon. Makes 4 to 6 servings.

Sweet Potato Ring with Cashews

Heavenly molded sweet potatoes for a buffet party table featuring baked ham. I am told by the Planters® test kitchen staff that this recipe is a favorite of Southern cooks, but you don't have to be Southern to enjoy it.

¼ cup firmly packed light brown sugar	1 cup milk
2 Tbs. Blue Bonnet® Margarine, melted	3 eggs
	1 tsp. ground cinnamon
¼ cup chopped Planters® Cashew Halves	½ tsp. salt
	¼ tsp. ground allspice
1 18-oz. can vacuum-packed sweet potatoes	

Combine brown sugar and Blue Bonnet® Margarine; spoon into bottom of a well-greased 1-quart ring mold. Arrange Planters® Cashew Halves in sugar mixture in mold. In electric blender or food processor combine sweet potatoes, milk, eggs, cinnamon, salt and allspice. Blend until smooth and creamy. Spoon into prepared ring mold. Place ring mold in pan of hot water and bake at 325°F. for 1 hour and 10 minutes, or until knife inserted in center comes out clean. Loosen edges with a knife; invert onto serving plate and serve immediately. Serves 6 to 8.

Sweet Potato Puffs

If you want to dress up sweet potatoes for company try this recipe from Blue Diamond® and the California Almond Grower Exchange. It's a classic from the 1950's.

3 large sweet potatoes	¼ cup brown sugar, packed
½ cup butter or margarine	⅛ tsp. pumpkin pie spice
½ cup milk	¼ cup blanched slivered Blue Diamond® Almonds
½ tsp. salt	

Scrub potatoes; cut off ends and place in baking pan. Bake in 400°F. (hot) oven 1 hour. Cut potatoes lengthwise into halves and scoop pulp into a mixing bowl. Add half the butter, then milk and salt. Beat until light and fluffy. Fill shells with potato mixture; return to oven. Cream together remaining butter, sugar and pumpkin pie spice. Fold in Almonds. Place a dollop of the almond topping on each potato half. Return to oven and heat five minutes or until topping is melted. Makes 6 servings.

Easy Corn Puff

A family favorite and definitely a "classic." During the 1950's it was featured in a recipe booklet packed in the Bisquick® Baking Mix box. So good!

2 10-oz. packages frozen
  corn or chopped broccoli
1 cup Bisquick® Baking Mix
1 cup milk

2 eggs
½ tsp. salt
1 cup shredded Cheddar
  cheese (about 4 ozs).

Heat oven to 325°F. Butter 5-cup soufflé dish or 1½-quart round casserole. Cook corn as directed on package; drain. Beat Baking Mix, milk, eggs and salt with hand beater until smooth. Stir in corn and cheese. Pour into soufflé dish. Bake until knife inserted halfway between center and edge comes out clean, about 1 hour. Serve immediately. Makes 6 servings.

Corn Pudding

In the 1960's Stokely–Van Camp® introduced this all-time favorite "new" recipe for creamed corn. It's an inspired combination of crispy whole kernel and old-fashioned cream-style corn.

1 Tbs. butter or margarine, melted
3 eggs, well-beaten
1 17-oz can Stokely's Finest® Whole Kernel Golden Corn, drained
1 17-oz can Stokely's Finest® Cream Style Golden Corn
2 Tbs. all-purpose flour
1 cup milk
1 tsp. sugar
½ tsp. salt
Dash pepper

Preheat oven to 350°F. Combine all ingredients. Pour into greased 1½-quart casserole. Place casserole in pan of water. Bake, uncovered, 1 hour and 20 minutes, or until knife inserted in center comes out clean. Makes 6 servings.

Confetti Green Beans

So easy, so elegant. This Italian-style recipe was printed on the inside label of the Land O Lakes® carton. It's really delicious.

⅓ cup Land O Lakes® Unsalted Butter
1 10-oz. package frozen cut green beans, thawed, drained
1 8-oz. can whole kernel corn, drained
½ cup pitted, sliced (¼-inch) ripe olives
1 tsp. *each* basil leaves and oregano leaves
½ tsp. garlic powder
1 medium tomato, cut into 16 wedges

In heavy 2-quart saucepan melt Butter over medium heat (4 to 5 minutes). Add remaining ingredients *except* tomato. Cover; cook over medium heat, stirring occasionally, until vegetables are crisply tender (8 to 10 minutes). Add tomato wedges. Cover; let stand 1 minute or until tomatoes are heated through. makes 4 1-cup servings.

Lemony Vegetable Sauté

This is one of my favorite vegetable combinations and everyone who tries it is delighted. It's very much like one my mother prepared, but this version, up-dated by Dole®, is just that little bit better.

½ lb. broccoli, cut into
   flowerettes
¼ cup oil
2 cups thinly sliced carrots
2 cups sliced Dole® Fresh
   Mushrooms

1 lemon, thinly sliced
¼ cup butter, melted
3 Tbs. sugar

Sauté broccoli in oil until tender-crisp. Remove. Stir in carrots and sauté until tender-crisp. Stir in mushrooms and sauté lightly. Return broccoli to skillet. Stir in lemon. Combine butter and sugar. Add to vegetables. Stir until vegetables are well glazed. Makes 4 to 6 servings.

Savory Baked Tomatoes

Here's the really delicious recipe from Pompeian® for baked stuffed tomatoes that people just keep asking for time and again.

4 large tomatoes
⅓ cup Pompeian® Olive Oil
1 small onion, chopped
1 pimiento, cut into strips
2 Tbs. minced ham

½ tsp. salt
⅛ tsp. pepper
¼ tsp. marjoram
1 Tbs. minced parsley
1 cup soft bread crumbs

Cut a 2-inch wide cap from the stem end of the tomatoes. Hollow out tomatoes, removing pulp and discard with the caps. Heat 4 Tbs. of olive oil in a skillet, add onion and sauté until tender. Stir in remaining ingredients, browning slightly. Spoon stuffing mixture into tomatoes. Place remaining 2 Tbs. olive oil into a shallow baking pan, arrange stuffed tomatoes in the pan, brush with a little of the oil. Bake at 350°F. for 40 minutes until cooked through. Makes 4 servings.

Creamed Cauliflower Casserole

An irresistible way to serve "good for you" vegetables. The recipe from the label of a classic convenience food— Pepperidge Farm® Stuffing Mix.

1 medium head cauliflower	1 8-oz. package Pepperidge Farm® Herb Seasoned Stuffing Mix
3 Tbs. butter or margarine	1 cup water
¼ cup flour	½ cup butter or margarine, melted
2 cups milk	
¾ tsp. salt	
⅛ tsp. pepper	

Break cauliflower into small pieces and cook until just tender. Drain and place in a shallow 2-quart casserole. Melt butter in a medium saucepan. Stir in flour and cook together a few minutes, while stirring. Remove from heat and blend in milk. Bring to a boil, stirring constantly, and simmer until thickened. Pour over cauliflower in casserole. Combine the last three ingredients and spoon on top, pressing down if necessary. Bake at 350°F. for 30 minutes. Serves 8 to 10.

Note: Broccoli used in place of cauliflower makes a delicious change.

Peas à la Crème

This vegetable dish always seems very special to me, partially because my mother often served it at luncheons and dinner parties, in little individual tart shells. It's Stokely–Van Camp's® alternate to just plain creamed peas.

⅓ cup commercial sour cream
½ tsp. instant chicken flavored bouillon
½ tsp. lemon juice
Dash pepper

1 16-oz. can Stokely's Finest® Peas
Fresh dill (optional)

Mix sour cream and bouillon in saucepan. Let stand 10 minutes to dissolve bouillon. Add lemon juice and pepper. Place over low heat to blend flavors; do not boil. Heat peas in their own liquid; drain. Place in serving dish; top with sauce, and garnish with fresh dill if desired. Makes 4 servings.

Broccoli au Gratin

Campbell's® way of making broccoli a party dish; a label recipe from my mother's time and one from Campbell's® 100 Best Recipes cookbook.

1 bunch broccoli (about 2 lbs.) or 1 small head cauliflower (or two 10-oz. frozen packages of either vegetable)
1 11-oz. can Campbell's® Condensed Cheddar Cheese soup

¼ cup milk
2 Tbs. buttered bread crumbs
4 slices bacon, cooked and crumbled

Cook vegatable; drain. Place in shallow baking dish (10 × 6 × 2 inches). Stir soup; blend in milk; pour over vegetable. Top with crumbs. Bake at 350°F. for 20 minutes or until hot. Garnish with bacon before serving. Makes 4 to 6 servings.

Cheese-Stuffed Zucchini

Even non-squash eaters will ask for seconds when you prepare this label recipe from Purity® Cheese.

8 medium zucchini, about 2¼ lbs.
1 package (8 ounces) May-Bud® Farmers Cheese, shredded
2 eggs, beaten
1 cup cooked rice
¼ cup finely chopped onion
¼ cup fine dry bread crumbs
1 Tbs. parsley flakes
½ tsp. salt
Seasoned salt
Paprika

Parboil zucchini for about 5 to 7 minutes. Cool. Cut in half lengthwise. Scoop out zucchini pulp, leaving shell. Place zucchini cut side down to drain. Chop pulp. Mix pulp with cheese, (reserving ½ cup) eggs, rice, onion, bread crumbs, parsley and salt. Sprinkle zucchini shells with seasoned salt; then stuff with cheese-rice mixture. Place in a greased 15½ × 10½ × 1-inch pan. Bake 350°F. for 20 to 25 minutes or until heated through. Last few minutes of baking top with remaining cheese. Makes 16 pieces.

Honey-Glazed Squash

A wintertime special at our house when I was a child and a classic recipe from the French® Company test kitchen.

2 or 3 acorn squash
  Salt and pepper
¼ cup honey
2 Tbs. butter or margarine,
  softened at room
  temperature
1 Tbs. French's®
  Worcestershire Sauce
¼ cup raisins

Cut squash in half; remove seeds. Place, cut-side down, in shallow pan; add about ½ inch hot water to pan. Bake in 350°F. oven 40 to 50 minutes, until almost tender. Discard water; turn squash cut-side up. Sprinkle with salt and pepper. Combine honey, butter, Worcestershire Sauce and raisins; spoon into cavities of squash. Return to oven and bake 15 minutes, until tender. Makes 4 to 6 servings.

French-Fried Onions

You'll never know how really great-tasting French-fried onions can be until you've fried your own. The "how to" is from the Crisco® Oil permanent recipe file. It's perfect.

2 large Bermuda onions
⅔ cup milk
½ cup all-purpose enriched
  flour
½ teaspoon salt
  Crisco® Oil for deep frying
  Salt

Cut cleaned onions into ¼-inch slices. Separate into rings. Soak onion rings in milk and then dip in flour seasoned with ½ tsp. salt. Fry a few at a time in deep Crisco® Oil heated to 375°F. Cook until lightly browned, 2 to 3 minutes. Drain on paper towels. Sprinkle with salt. Makes about 4 servings.

Monterey Bay Chutney

I couldn't quite decide where to place this Sun-Maid® recipe; it's more a relish than a side dish, but it goes well with roast chicken, lamb chops or steak and it tastes so great that it just had to be included somewhere in the book.

1 cup Sun-Maid® Seedless Raisins
1 cup Sun-Maid® Golden Seedless Raisins
1 cup Sun-Maid® Currants
1 cup finely chopped onion
1 quart diced pared tart apples
1 tsp. salt
1½ tsps. powdered ginger
½ tsp. allspice
⅛ tsp. cloves
1 cup vinegar
1 cup dry white wine or water
½ cup sugar
¼ cup diced green pepper
¼ cup diced pimiento

Combine all ingredients, except green pepper and pimiento. Simmer 20 to 25 minutes, uncovered, until thickened. Add green pepper and pimiento. Cook 5 minutes longer. Cool. Makes about 1½ quarts.

6.
As Good as Bread

Just a few weeks after I started collecting recipes for this book I tested one of the breads—Portuguese Sweet Bread (the fourth recipe in this section). After reading the list of ingredients I thought this might be the type bread my family and I like most, and it was. Richly flavored, with a firm but light texture, it was delicious, a superb loaf. As we sat at the kitchen table eating thick, still slightly warm slices spread with sweet creamy butter and enjoying a freshly made pot of coffee I realized more than ever why the Spanish say "bueno como el pan" ("as good as bread") for a superlative compliment. There really isn't anything better but there are many people in this country who have never even tasted, and certainly not made, a loaf of home-baked bread.

It's a pity, but I think I understand why: they think breadmaking is a difficult, time-consuming job, only successful for the very experienced cook. Well, that may have been true back in the days when the stove was heated by wood, and flour came in just two ways; with weevils and without, but it's no longer so. These days breadmaking is not only easy, it can be relaxing and fun. Now that we can select just the right flour for the particular type bread we want to bake, and the yeast is never stale, and now that the recipe has been tested and perfected for us with all the guesswork taken out, a loaf of honest home-baked bread is no more difficult than cookies or cake. In fact it's usually easier. That's especially true of the recipes in this book. Not one of them takes more than a half hour of actual work time (yeast breads do the job of rising all by themselves), and many take less. More importantly, you are going to love the results. The heavenly aroma (nothing is quite as tantalizing as the smell of freshly baked bread) and the sheer joy of eating are well worth the small effort it takes.

I wish I could tell you which bread I like best in this collection, but I simply cannot. There are at least a dozen I can call my favorites. I can't help loving the light but rich old-fashioned Southern Biscuits; no matter how often I'm told if I add "that much butter and strawberry jam besides" they are, in a word, too high in calories. On the other hand my fondness for healthy, super-nutritious Bran Yeast Bread remains constant. I could, and often do, make a meal of a thick, freshly made slice.

Another time my favorite would be any one of the rich and pleasantly sweet coffee cakes, or the Sour-Cream Pecan Tea Ring, almost a cake but not quite, or the Coconut Breakfast Bread served warm. But then they are *all* my favorites—they are all *bueno como el pan*, as good as only bread can be. Just try them yourself.

Delicious White Bread

Here's a classic "label" recipe from Pillsbury® that is very simple to make, yet is beautiful to look at and eat.

5 to 6 cups Pillsbury's® Best
  Bread Flour
3 Tbs. sugar
2 tsps. salt

2 packages active dry yeast
2 cups water
¼ cup oil or shortening

Grease two 8 × 4-inch or 9 × 5-inch loaf pans. Lightly spoon flour into measuring cup; level off. In large bowl, combine 2 cups flour, sugar, salt and yeast; blend well. In small saucepan, heat water and oil until very warm (120°F. to 130°F.). Add warm liquid to flour mixture. Blend at low speed until moistened; beat 3 minutes at medium speed. By hand, stir in 2½ to 3 cups flour until dough pulls cleanly away from sides of bowl. On floured surface, knead in ½ to 1 cup flour until dough is smooth and elastic with blisters under the surface, about 10 minutes. Place dough in greased bowl; cover loosely with plastic wrap and cloth towel. Let rise in warm place until light and doubled in size, about 1½ hours. Punch down dough several times to remove all air bubbles. Divide dough into 2 parts; mold into balls. Allow to rest on counter, covered with inverted bowl, for 15 minutes. Work dough with hands to remove large air bubbles. Shape into two loaves. Place in prepared pans. Cover; let rise in warm place until dough fills pans and tops of loaves are about 1 inch above pan edges, about 1 hour. Heat oven to 375°F. Bake for 45 to 55 minutes until loaves sound hollow when lightly tapped. Remove from pans immediately; cool on wire racks. If desired, for soft crusts brush tops of loaves with melted butter. Makes 2 loaves.

Buttermilk Bread

This back-of-the-label recipe, almost as old as the Fleischmann's® first test kitchen, has been updated and simplified, but the flavor remains as homey good as your grandmother's bread.

6 cups unsifted flour
(about)
3 Tbs. sugar
2½ tsps. salt
¼ tsp. baking soda
1 package Fleischmann's®
Active Dry Yeast
1 cup buttermilk
1 cup water
⅓ cup margarine

Combine 2 cups flour, sugar, salt, baking soda and undissolved yeast. Heat buttermilk, water and margarine over low heat until liquids are warm. (Mixture will appear curdled.) Add to dry ingredients; beat for 2 minutes at medium speed, scraping bowl occasionally. Add 1 cup flour. Beat at high speed for 2 minutes. Stir in enough flour to make a soft dough. Turn onto floured board; knead about 8 to 10 minutes. Place in greased bowl; grease top. Cover; let rise until doubled, about 1 hour. Punch down; turn onto floured board. Divide dough in half. Shape into loaves. Place each in a greased 8½ × 4½ × 2½-inch loaf pan. Cover; let rise until doubled, about 1 hour. Bake at 375°F. about 35 minutes, or until done. Remove from pans and cool on wire racks. Makes 2 loaves.

Quick Buttermilk Rolls

What could be easier than baking these prize-winning buttermilk yeast rolls? Alberta Beaty, who developed the recipe for a Red Star® Baking Contest, says they are both easy and delicious. Seems the judges agreed.

4 to 4½ cups all-purpose
    flour
2 packages Red Star®
    Instant Blend Dry Yeast
3 Tbs. sugar

1 tsp. salt
½ tsp. soda
1¼ cups buttermilk
½ cup water
½ cup shortening

Preheat oven to 400°F. In large mixer bowl, combine 1½ cups flour, yeast, sugar, salt and soda; mix well. In saucepan, heat buttermilk, water and shortening until warm (120°F. to 130°F., shortening does not need to melt). Add to flour mixture. Blend at low speed until moistened; beat 3 minutes at medium speed. By hand, gradually stir in enough remaining flour to make a firm dough. Knead on floured surface until smooth and elastic, about 5 minutes. Place in greased bowl, turning to grease top. Cover; let rise in warm place until light and doubled, about 20 minutes. Punch down dough. Divide dough into 24 pieces. Form into balls; place on greased cookie sheet or 15 × 10-inch pan. Cover; let rise in warm place until almost doubled, about 20 minutes. Bake at 400°F. for 15 to 20 minutes until golden brown. Remove from pan; brush with butter, if desired. Cool on racks. Makes 24 rolls.

Portuguese Sweet Bread

This is one of my favorite breads, and everyone who tries it is as pleased as I am with its just slightly sweet taste and light

texture. It was featured on the back of Fleischmann's® Yeast package a few years ago and requests are so frequent it may be put back there again next season.

6¼ cups (about) unsifted flour
⅔ cup sugar
1 tsp. grated lemon peel
¼ tsp. ground mace
1 package Fleischmann's® Active Dry Yeast
⅔ cup potato water

½ cup milk
½ cup margarine
3 eggs (at room temperature)
½ cup unseasoned mashed potato
Confectioners sugar

Combine 1½ cups flour, sugar, lemon peel, mace and undissolved yeast. Heat potato water, milk and margarine to 120°F. to 130°F. Add to dry ingredients; beat 2 minutes. Add eggs, mashed potato and ½ cup flour. Beat 2 minutes. Stir in more flour to make a soft dough. On floured board, knead 8 to 10 minutes. Place in greased bowl; turn to grease top. Cover; let rise until doubled, about 1¾ hours. Punch dough down, roll out to 16 × 10 inches. Roll up. Place, seam side down, in greased 10-inch tube pan. Pinch ends to form ring. Cover; let rise until doubled, about 1 hour. Bake at 350°F. 40 minutes or until done. Cool in pan 5 minutes. Remove. Cool. Dust with confectioners sugar.

Bran Yeast Loaf

If your mother or grandmother saved the Kellogg's® box the original version of this recipe appeared on, she would have a collectors' item. It was decorated with one of a series of illustrations by Norman Rockwell; the recipe alone is a collectors' item.

2 packages active dry yeast	2 tsps. salt
2¼ cups warm water (110°F. to 115°F.)	5½ cups all-purpose flour
⅓ cup molasses	3 cups Kellogg's® 40% Bran Flakes® Cereal
2 Tbs. vegetable oil	2 Tbs. margarine or butter, melted

Dissolve yeast in warm water in large mixing bowl. Add molasses, oil, salt and 3 cups of the flour. Beat well. Stir in cereal. Add remaining flour to make a stiff dough. On lightly floured surface, knead dough about 10 minutes or until smooth and elastic. Place in greased bowl, turning once to grease top. Cover lightly. Let rise in warm place until double in volume (about 1 hour). Punch down dough. Let rest 15 minutes. Shape into 2 loaves and placed in greased 9 × 5 × 3-inch loaf pans. Brush with melted margarine. Cover and let rise in warm place until double in volume (about 30 minutes). Bake at 375°F. about 45 minutes or until golden brown. Remove from pans and cool on wire rack. Makes 2 loaves.

Whole Wheat Potato Bread

Another updated classic from Pillsbury®. My favorite friend says it's even good eaten plain, without butter; you may agree.

3½ cups Pillsbury's® Best Bread Flour	1½ cups water
1½ cups Hungry Jack® Mashed Potato Flakes	1¼ cups milk
2½ tsps. salt	¼ cup margarine or butter
2 packages active dry yeast	¼ cup honey
	2 eggs
	2½ to 3 cups Pillsbury's® Best Whole Wheat Flour

Grease two 8 × 4- or 9 × 5-inch loaf pans. Lightly spoon flour into measuring cup; level off. In large bowl, combine 2 cups bread flour, potato flakes, salt and yeast; blend well. In medium saucepan, heat water, milk, margarine and honey until very warm (120° to 130°F.). Add warm liquid and eggs to flour mixture. Blend at low speed until moistened; beat 4 minutes at medium speed. By hand, stir in 1½ cups bread flour and 1½ to 2 cups whole wheat flour until dough pulls cleanly away from sides of bowl. On floured surface, knead in remaining 1 to 1½ cups whole wheat flour until dough is smooth and elastic, about 10 minutes. Place dough in greased bowl, cover loosely with plastic wrap and cloth towel. Let rise in warm place until light and doubled in size, about 1½ hours. Punch down dough. Divide dough into two parts; mold into balls. Allow to rest on counter, covered with inverted bowl, for 15 minutes. Shape dough into 2 loaves; place in prepared pans. Cover; let rise in warm place until doubled in size, about 1 hour. Heat oven to 375°F. Bake loaves for 35 to 40 minutes or until deep golden brown and loaves sound hollow when lightly tapped. Immediately remove loaves from pans. If desired, brush with margarine or butter. Makes 2 loaves.

Ralston Whole Wheat Bread

This recipe for Ralston® Whole Wheat Bread has been revised, but it still has the same good flavor of the original one developed almost 30 years ago. Try toasting it for a real treat.

2¼ cups Instant or Regular Ralston® cereal
¼ cup sugar
1 Tbs. salt
⅓ cup vegetable shortening
4 cups (1 quart) milk, scalded
2 packages active dry yeast
½ cup warm water
7 to 8 cups all-purpose flour

Grease 3 8½ × 4½ × 2½-inch loaf pans. Combine Ralston®, sugar, salt and shortening in large bowl. Add hot, scalded milk. Stir until thoroughly moistened. Cool to warm (105°F. to 115°F.), stirring occasionally. Dissolve yeast in water. Stir into cereal mixture. Add 2 cups flour. Mix well. Gradually stir in enough additional flour to form a stiff dough. Place on floured surface. Knead until smooth and elastic (8 to 10 minutes). Work in additional flour as needed. Form into ball. Place in greased bowl. Turn to grease all sides. Cover. Let rise in warm place, free from draft, until double (about 1 hour). Punch dough down. Place on lightly floured surface. Knead about 2 minutes. Divide dough in thirds. Form into loaves. Place in pans. Cover. Let rise in warm place until almost double (about 30 minutes). Bake in preheated 400°F. oven about 30 minutes or until browned and bread sounds hollow when lightly tapped. Remove from pans at once. Cool on rack. Makes 3 loaves. Use 1 loaf fresh from the oven. Freeze two to enjoy later.

Note: For golden brown, shiny top, brush tops with beaten egg before baking.

Russian Black Bread

This hearty "old country" loaf has been a specialty of whole-grain bakers for almost 20 years. Fleischmann's® Yeast put it on their package label that long ago.

1 cup unsifted rye flour
2 to 2½ cups unsifted white flour
½ cup whole bran cereal
2 tsps. caraway seed, crushed
1 tsp. salt
½ tsp. sugar
½ tsp. instant coffee
½ tsp. onion powder
¼ tsp. fennel seed, crushed
1 package Fleischmann's® Active Dry Yeast
1 cup water
2 Tbs. white vinegar
2 Tbs. dark molasses
2 Tbs. Fleischmann's® Margarine
½ square (½ oz.) unsweetened chocolate
½ tsp. corn starch
¼ cup cold water

Combine rye and white flours. In a large bowl thoroughly mix 2 cups flour mixture with cereal, caraway seed, salt, sugar, instant coffee, onion powder, fennel seed and Fleischmann's® Active Dry Yeast. Combine 1 cup water, vinegar, molasses, Fleischmann's® Margarine and chocolate in a saucepan and heat over low heat until liquids are very warm (120°F. to 130°F.). Margarine and chocolate do not need to melt. Gradually add to dry ingredients and beat 2 minutes at medium speed of electric mixer, scraping bowl occasionally. Stir in enough additional flour mixture to make a soft dough. Turn out onto lightly floured board. Knead until smooth and elastic, 5 to 7 minutes. Cover; let rise in a warm place, free from draft, until doubled in bulk, about 1 hour. Bake at 350°F. for 45 to 50 minutes, or until done. Meanwhile, combine corn starch and cold water. Cook over medium heat, stirring constantly 1 minute. As soon as loaf is baked, brush corn starch mixture over top. Return bread to oven and bake 2 minutes longer, or until glaze is set. Remove from pan and cool on wire rack. Makes 1 loaf.

Coconut Breakfast Breads

This is bread for a special breakfast—Christmas morning maybe or New Year's Day. The Holland House® people recommend you make it any day to make the next morning a special one.

⅓ cup milk, scalded
¾ stick unsalted butter
½ cup Coco Casa® Cream of Coconut
1 tsp. vanilla extract
¾ tsp. salt
3 large eggs, lightly beaten

1 package dry active yeast, dissolved in 2 Tbs. warm water
4 cups unbleached flour
1 egg yolk mixed in 3 Tbs. water for glaze (below)

Filling
Stir together to form a paste

½ cup Coco Casa® Cream of Coconut
4 Tbs. coconut flakes

4 Tbs. chocolate bits or
4 Tbs. ground toasted almonds

Stir butter in scalded milk until dissolved. Add Cream of Coconut, vanilla and salt. Place eggs in bowl with milk mixture, yeast and flour. Knead until dough is pliable and satiny to the touch, adding more flour if necessary. Place in large buttered bowl. Cover with buttered foil. Let rise in warm place 2½ to 3 hours until it triples in volume. Punch down and shape into brioches or a loaf.

Brioches
Butter 12 small brioche molds. Flatten into a 4-inch circle enough dough to half fill mold. Place 1 Tbs. filling in center, fold into a cushion and place, seam down, in mold. Cut a cross on surface, and into this press a ball of dough the size of a walnut.

Loaf

Butter a 5 × 9-inch loaf pan. Roll dough in a 9-inch square. Spread filling evenly over surface, roll tightly and place seam down into pan.

Glaze for either loaf or brioche

Let dough rise again for 1 to 1½ hours or until doubled. Brush with egg glaze. Bake in preheated 400°F. oven. Brioches: 30 to 35 minutes. Loaf: 50 to 60 minutes.

Grandma's Cinnamon Rolls

A German grandmother from Minnesota passed on the recipe for these delicious rolls to Barbara Hawkins of Denton, Kansas, who entered them in a Red Star® Baking Contest. The "secret" that makes them special is the coffee and maple flavoring in the icing which is spread on the still warm rolls.

5½ to 6 cups all-purpose flour
2 packages Red Star® Instant Blend Dry Yeast
½ cup sugar
1½ tsps. salt
1 cup milk
1 cup water

¼ cup butter or margarine
2 eggs
⅓ cup butter or margarine, melted
¾ cup sugar
1½ tsps. cinnamon
½ cup chopped nuts

Glaze

3 Tbs. butter or margarine, melted
2 cups powdered sugar
3 to 4 Tbs. hot coffee
½ tsp. maple flavor

Preheat oven 375°F. In large mixer bowl, combine 2 cups flour, yeast, ½ cup sugar and salt; mix well. In saucepan, heat milk, water and butter until warm (120°F. to 130°F.; butter does not need to melt). Add to flour mixture. Add eggs. Blend at low speed until moistened; beat 3 minutes at medium speed. By hand, gradually stir in enough remaining flour to make a soft dough. Knead on floured surface until smooth and elastic, about 5 minutes. Place in greased bowl, turning to grease top. Cover; let rise in warm place until light and doubled, about 1 hour. Punch down dough. Divide into 2 parts. On lightly floured surface, roll or pat each half into a 12 × 9-inch rectangle. Brush each part with melted butter. Combine ¾ cup sugar, cinnamon and nuts. Sprinkle over butter. Starting with shorter side, roll up tightly, pressing dough into roll with each turn. Pinch edges to seal. Cut each roll into 12 pieces. Place cut-side down in greased 13 × 9-inch pans. Cover; let rise in warm place until almost doubled, about 30 minutes. Bake at 375°F. for 20 minutes until golden brown. Combine Glaze ingredients; blend until smooth. Drizzle over hot rolls. Cool on racks. Makes 24 rolls.

Viennese Crescent Ring

Talk about good cooks, this elegant coffee cake won a special 1980 contest held for three-time Bake Off® Finalists who were no longer eligible for Pillsbury's regular yearly contest.

1 cup finely ground almonds
⅓ cup powdered sugar
2 Tbs. margarine or butter, softened
1 tsp. almond extract

1 egg yolk (reserve egg white for topping)
2 8-oz. cans Pillsbury® Refrigerated Crescent Dinner Quick Rolls

Topping

⅓ cup apricot preserves
⅓ cup pineapple preserves
   Reserved egg white
¼ cup sliced unblanched almonds
 1 Tbs. sugar

Heat oven to 350°F. In medium bowl, combine ground almonds, powdered sugar, margarine, almond extract and egg yolk; blend well. (Mixture will be stiff.) Set aside. Separate one can of dough into 4 rectangles. Place in ungreased 12-inch pizza pan; press over bottom, sealing perforations. Separate second can of dough into 8 triangles. Spread 1 rounded Tbs. of almond filling over each triangle. Roll up; start at shortest side of triangle and roll to opposite point. Arrange filled crescents, pointed-side-down, evenly around edge of dough-lined pan. In small bowl, combine preserves. Spoon evenly over center of dough spreading just to filled rolls. Beat egg white until frothy; brush over tops of filled crescents. Sprinkle with sliced almonds; sprinkle sugar evenly over almonds. Bake at 350°F. for 25 to 30 minutes or until golden brown. Cut into wedges to serve. Serve warm. Makes 8 servings.

Pita Bread

Another great recipe from Pillsbury® that deserves a gold star. These tender, crisp rolls are super easy to bring freshly baked to the table.

¾ cup boiling water
 2 Tbs. margarine or butter, softened
 1 package Pillsbury® Hot Roll Mix

Cornmeal
Milk, if desired
Sesame seeds, if desired

Measure boiling water into large bowl; stir in margarine until completely melted. Sprinkle with yeast packet from Hot Roll mix; stir until dissolved. Add flour mixture; blend well. Knead dough on lightly floured surface for about 2 minutes until smooth. Cover; let rise in a warm place until doubled in size, 30 to 45 minutes. Lightly sprinkle cornmeal onto 2 ungreased cookie sheets. Divide dough into 6 equal pieces; shape into balls. On lightly floured surface, roll each piece into a 7-inch circle. Place 3 circles on each cookie sheet. Let rise again in warm place, 30 to 45 minutes, until light and slightly risen. For sesame seed pita bread, brush circles with small amount of milk and sprinkle lightly with sesame seeds. Bake in preheated 425°F. oven for 5 to 10 minutes or until light golden brown. Cut in half crosswise and slice to form pocket before storing. Makes 6 pita breads, 12 servings.

Sunland Vineyard Loaf

Super-good and super-quick, this raisin bread made from packaged hot roll mix made its debut in a Sun-Maid® booklet back in 1977. The recipe says to cool it, but I must admit I can't wait, so it's always served still slightly warm at our house.

1 cup Sun-Maid® Seedless
  Raisins
⅓ cup sherry
1 13¾-oz. package hot roll
  mix
¼ cup warm water
½ cup hot milk

2 Tbs. butter
1 Tbs. sugar
1 egg, beaten
½ cup chopped walnuts
4 bay leaves (optional)
  Melted butter

Chop raisins coarsely; add sherry. Let stand an hour or more. Dissolve yeast from mix in warm water. Combine milk, butter and sugar; when lukewarm, add yeast and egg. Beat in flour mixture from package. Mix in walnuts and drained raisins. Cover, and let rise in warm place until doubled, 1¼ to 1½ hours. Punch down. Divide into 8 portions. Shape each into a slender roll 8 inches long. Twist 2 together for each loaf; fit into greased pans, 5½ × 3 inches, with a bay leaf in bottom of pan. Brush with melted butter. Let rise until doubled, 30 to 40 minutes. Bake on low shelf at 375°F. 30 to 35 minutes. Turn out and cool.

Banana Nut Bread

This moist, well-textured bread was first used in a Wheat Chex® Cereal recipe book about 20 years ago. It's included in that company's all-time great recipe file.

1½ cups all-purpose flour
½ cup sugar
2½ tsps. baking powder
½ tsp. salt
½ tsp. baking soda
1 cup Wheat Chex® Cereal
  crushed to ½ cup

⅓ cup chopped nuts
1 egg, slightly beaten
¼ cup vegetable oil
2 Tbs. water
1½ cups mashed banana
  (3 large)
1 tsp. vanilla

Preheat oven to 350°F. Grease an 8½ × 4½ × 2½-inch loaf pan. Stir together flour, sugar, baking powder, salt, baking soda, Wheat Chex Cereal® and nuts. Combine egg, oil, water, mashed banana and vanilla. Add all at once to dry ingredients. Stir just until moistened. Spread evenly into pan. Bake 50 to 55 minutes or until tester inserted in center comes out clean. Let cool 15 minutes before removing from pan. Makes 1 loaf.

Note: May be baked in three 5¾ × 3¼ × 2-inch loaf pans (bake about 40 minutes) or six 4½ × 2½ × 1¼-inch loaf pans (bake about 30 minutes).

Fruit and Cereal Brunch Cake

From the General Mills® kitchens, an adaptation of a classic German recipe. Serve this rich coffee cake at breakfast, brunch or tea time.

2 cups Total® Cereal
1 cup orange juice
¼ cup vegetable oil
1 egg
2 medium bananas, mashed
1½ cups Gold Medal® All-Purpose Flour

¾ cup sugar
½ cup raisins, if desired
1 tsp. baking soda
1 tsp. ground cinnamon
½ tsp. salt
Streusel Topping (below)

Heat oven to 350°F. Grease square pan, 9 × 9 × 2-inches. Mix cereal and orange juice in large bowl; let stand until softened, about 2 minutes. Mix in oil, egg and bananas. Stir in flour, sugar, raisins, baking soda, cinnamon and salt. Spread in pan. Bake until top springs back when touched, 40 to 45 minutes. Sprinkle Streusel Topping over warm coffee cake. Set oven control to broil and/or 550°F. Broil with top about 5 inches from heat until bubbly, about 1 minute. (Watch carefully to avoid burning.) Makes 9 to 12 servings.

Streusel Topping

½ cup packed brown sugar
½ cup chopped nuts
¼ cup Gold Medal All-Purpose Flour

¼ cup margarine or butter, softened
½ tsp. ground cinnamon

Mix all ingredients until crumbly.

Honeycomb Coffee Cake

Who doesn't like warm, fragrant buttery coffee cake sweetened with honey? A featured recipe on the inside label of Land O Lakes® Unsalted Butter. It's a treasure.

1¾ cups all-purpose flour
½ cup sugar
½ cup Land O Lakes® Unsalted Butter, softened
⅓ cup milk

2 eggs
2 tsp. baking powder
½ tsp. almond extract
½ tsp. orange extract
Topping (below)

Preheat oven to 350°F. Grease 9-inch square baking pan. In 3-quart mixer bowl combine all coffee cake ingredients. Beat at medium speed, scraping sides of bowl often, until well mixed (1 to 2 minutes). Spread into greased pan. Set aside. In heavy 2-quart saucepan combine all topping ingredients. Cook over medium heat, stirring occasionally, until mixture comes to a full boil (5 to 6 minutes). Continue cooking, stirring occasionally, until mixture boils (2 to 3 minutes). Pour topping evenly over coffee cake. Bake near center at 350°F. oven for 22 to 27 minutes or until wooden pick inserted in center comes out clean. Makes 1 9-inch square coffee cake.

Topping

½ cup Land O Lakes® Unsalted Butter
½ cup chopped pecans
¼ cup sugar
¼ cup honey
½ tsp. nutmeg
1 Tbs. milk
½ tsp. orange extract

Top-Stove Coffee Cake

In 1947 the Pet® Milk Company published an up-dated edition of their original 1932 *Gold Cookbook*. This recipe was included, and it's still on their most frequently requested list.

1 cup sifted all-purpose flour	1 well-beaten egg
⅓ cup sugar	⅓ cup Pet® Milk
2 tsp. baking powder	⅓ cup water
¾ tsp. cinnamon	3 Tbs. melted shortening
½ tsp. salt	¼ cup sugar
	¾ tsp. cinnamon

Grease a heavy 9-inch skillet. Cover the bottom with 1 layer of heavy brown wrapping paper cut to fit. Grease top layer of paper. Sift together first 5 ingredients into bowl. Mix together the egg, Pet® Milk, water and shortening. Add, all at once, to flour mixture; mix quickly but thoroughly. Pour into prepared skillet. Sprinkle with a mixture of ¼ cup sugar and ¾ tsp. cinnamon. Cover and bake on top of range over very low heat 30 minutes, or until firm to the touch. Lift out carefully and remove paper while still hot. Decorate with shelled walnut halves, if desired. Serve warm or cold. Makes one 9-inch cake.

Note: To bake this cake in the oven, omit paper, place uncovered skillet on center shelf of a moderate oven (375°F.). Bake 25 minutes or until firm to the touch.

Mexican Corn Bread

This very different corn bread has been a favorite of Mrs. W. B. Stokely, III, for years; it is a much-requested recipe from the Stokely–Van Camp® test kitchens.

1⅓ cups yellow cornmeal
1⅓ cups all-purpose flour
3 Tbs. sugar
½ tsp. baking soda
1 tsp. salt
2 eggs
1 cup buttermilk
1 8½-oz. can Stokely's® Finest® Cream Style Golden Corn

2 Tbs. bacon drippings
1 medium-size onion, finely chopped
6 strips bacon, cooked and crumbled
¾ cup grated American cheese, divided
1 to 2 Tbs. chopped green chilies

Preheat oven to 400°F. Butter 9-inch square pan. Combine cornmeal, flour, sugar, baking soda and salt in large mixing bowl. Beat eggs and stir in buttermilk, Corn, bacon drippings, onion, bacon, ½ cup cheese and chilies. Add to cornmeal mixture; stir until well combined. Pour batter into prepared pan and sprinkle with remaining ¼ cup cheese. Bake 45 minutes. Makes 8 to 10 servings.

Cinnamon Apple Rolls

These rolls belong to the "sticky bun" family, of which I am an avid fan. You will be too when you try them. The recipe was developed by the Crisco® Oil people and it's one of their all-time most requested.

3 cups sifted all-purpose enriched flour
2 Tbs. sugar
4 tsps. double-acting baking powder
1 tsp. salt
1 cup milk
½ cup Crisco® Oil

2 cups chopped, pared apples
½ cup brown sugar
1 tsp. cinnamon
1 cup brown sugar
½ cup Crisco® Oil
½ cup chopped nuts

Combine flour, 2 Tbs. sugar, baking powder and salt. Add milk and ½ cup Crisco® Oil; stir just enough to hold dough together. Place on lightly floured surface and knead 10 to 12 strokes. Roll to ¼-inch thick rectangle. Cover dough with combined apples, ½ cup brown sugar and cinnamon. Roll up jelly-roll fashion. Cut into 1-inch thick pieces. Combine 1 cup brown sugar, ½ cup Crisco® Oil and nuts in bottom of 13 × 9 × 2-inch pan. Place rolls in pan. Bake at 425°F. for 15 to 20 minutes, until desired brownness. Immediately turn upside down onto large platter or cookie sheet. Serve warm. Makes about 8 rolls.

Bran Nut and Raisin Bread

The first in-flight meal to be served aboard a passenger plane took place on April 8, 1930. Fifteen presidents of Detroit women's organizations were served a luncheon prepared by Mary I. Barber, home economic director at the Kellogg® Company. It was a cooperative venture; Kellogg's® supplied the meal, and the Ford Motor Company provided the "Tin Goose" tri-motor club plane. A report on the outing stated that the Bran Nut and Raisin Bread was especially well received and, oh yes, the women enjoyed the flight.

1½ cups all-purpose flour
 1 Tbs. baking powder
 1 tsp. salt
1½ cups Kellogg's®
    All-Bran® Cereal
 ⅓ cup firmly packed brown
    sugar

¾ cup milk
¾ cup water
⅓ cup molasses
¾ cup English walnuts,
    broken
¾ cup seedless raisins

Stir together flour, baking powder and salt. Set aside. In large mixing bowl, mix together cereal, sugar, milk, water and molasses. Mix in flour mixture. Stir in walnuts and raisins. Spread in greased 9 × 5 × 3-inch loaf pan. Bake at 350°F. about 1 hour until wooden pick inserted near center comes out clean. Makes 1 loaf.

Saffron Loaves

Start the week off right with this bread. Monday won't look so bad and the rest of the week will look better when you treat yourself and friends to this delicious sunny-colored, sunny-tasting Dole® Banana Loaf.

1 cup butter	4 tsps. baking powder
1 cup sugar	1 tsp. salt
3 eggs, separated	⅛ tsp. saffron*
2 medium ripe Dole®	1 cup seedless raisins
bananas	½ cup coarsely chopped
1 cup milk	peanuts
3½ cups flour	

Cream butter and sugar until light and fluffy. Beat in egg yolks until blended. Mash bananas to make 1 cup. Combine with milk. Combine remaining ingredients. Add to creamed mixture alternately with milk mixture until blended. Beat egg whites until stiff peaks form, but not dry. Fold into batter. Pour into two 8 × 4 × 2½-inch well-greased loaf pans. Bake in a 350°F. oven 50 to 60 minutes until cake tests done. Cool 10 minutes. Invert onto wire racks to complete cooling. Makes 2 loaves.

* Substitute 2 tsps. cinnamon

Biscuits

Remember Scarlett "stuffin'" biscuits before the big barbecue at Twelve Oaks? The recipe for these absolutely authentic Southern biscuits was one of the first to appear on the Pillsbury® self-rising flour bag. It's a classic for sure.

2 cups Pillsbury's® Best Self-Rising or
   Unbleached Self-Rising Flour
½ cup shortening
¾ cup milk

Heat oven to 450°F. Lightly spoon flour into measuring cup; level off. Cut shortening into flour with fork until consistency of coarse meal. Add milk all at once; stir with fork just until a soft dough forms. Turn dough onto lightly floured surface; sprinkle dough lightly with flour. Knead gently 10 times or until no longer sticky. Roll out dough to ½-inch thickness; cut with 2-inch floured biscuit cutter. Place biscuits on ungreased cookie sheet. Bake at 450°F. for 8 to 12 minutes or until golden brown. Makes 12 biscuits.

Variations:

Crispy Biscuits: Roll out dough to ⅛- to ¼-inch thickness. Cut with floured 2¾-inch biscuit cutter. Bake at 425°F. for 8 to 10 minutes.

Buttermilk Biscuits: Substitute buttermilk for milk. Add ¼ tsp. soda.

Sausage or Bacon Biscuits: Fry ½ lb. sausage or bacon. Drain well; crumble. Add to flour-shortening mixture. Refrigerate leftovers.

Cheese Biscuits: Add 8 oz. (2 cups) shredded Cheddar cheese to flour-shortening mixture.

Cornmeal Biscuits: Substitute ½ cup cornmeal for ½ cup flour.

Drop Biscuits: Increase milk to 1 cup. Drop dough by tablespoonfuls onto greased cookie sheet.

Irish Soda Bread

A favorite recipe featured on the Bisquick box in the 1970's and in Betty Crocker's® "Creative Recipes" booklet. Best served warm (not hot), cut into wedges, split and spread with soft butter.

4 cups Bisquick® Baking Mix
1 cup Gold Medal® Whole Wheat Flour
3 Tbs. sugar

¼ cup firm margarine or butter
2 eggs
1½ cups buttermilk

Heat oven to 350°F. Generously grease 1½-quart round casserole. Mix baking mix, flour and sugar in large bowl. Cut in margarine until crumbly. Beat eggs slightly; reserve 1 Tbs. Stir remaining eggs and the buttermilk into crumbly mixture until moistened. Turn dough onto well-floured cloth-covered board. Knead 20 times. Shape dough into ball; place in casserole. Cut 4-inch cross about ¼-inch deep in center of ball. Brush dough with reserved egg. Bake until wooden pick inserted in center comes out clean, 60 to 70 minutes. Cool 10 minutes; remove from casserole. Makes 1 loaf.

Peanut Butter Wheat Crackers

Quick, easy and absolutely delicious; a must-have, much-requested recipe from the Skippy® Peanut Butter kitchens.

1 cup unsifted flour	1 cup Skippy® Super
1 cup unsifted	Chunk Peanut Butter
whole-wheat flour	½ cup (about) water
¼ cup wheat germ	2 Tbs. cider vinegar
1½ tsps. caraway seeds	Milk
1 tsp. salt	Coarse salt (optional)
½ tsp. baking soda	

In large bowl mix together flour, whole-wheat flour, wheat germ, caraway seeds, salt and baking soda. With pastry blender or two knives, cut in Peanut Butter until coarse crumbs form. Add water and vinegar; mix until dough holds together (if mixture is too dry additional water may be added 1 Tbs. at a time). Divide dough in half. On lightly floured surface roll half of dough out to ⅛-inch thickness. Cut with 3-inch round cookie cutter. Repeat with scraps and remaining half of dough. Place on ungreased cookie sheet. Brush surface with milk. If desired, sprinkle with coarse salt. Bake in 375°F. oven 13 to 15 minutes or until browned and crisp. Remove from pan and cool on wire racks. Store in airtight container. Makes about 40 crackers.

Whole Wheat Cheese Wafers

In 1907 the Kellogg Company ran a promotion campaign with newspaper advertisements that read, "Give the grocer a wink, and see what you get: KTC." KTC stood for Kellogg's® Toasted Corn Flakes® and every customer who winked at the grocer received a free cereal sample. In New York City alone sales increased from two railroad carloads monthly to a car-

load a day! A more recent but less-daring promotion featured this recipe for these delicious cheese wafers.

½ cup margarine or butter, softened
2 cups (8 ozs.) shredded sharp Cheddar cheese
3 cups Kellogg's® Rice Krispies® cereal, crushed to measure 1½ cups
¾ cup whole wheat flour

In large mixing bowl, beat margarine and cheese until very light and fluffy. Stir in crushed Cereal. Add flour, mixing until well combined. Portion dough using rounded measuring teaspoon. Shape into balls. Place on ungreased baking sheets. Flatten with fork dipped in flour. Bake at 350°F. about 12 minutes or until lightly browned around edges. Remove immediately from baking sheets. Cool on wire racks. Makes about 7 dozen.

Surprise Muffins

These easy-to-make muffins made their debut back in the 1950's when the recipe appeared in a national Welsh® Concord Grape Jelly ad. Their homey, old-fashioned flavor is just right with freshly made coffee.

3 cups sifted all-purpose flour
4 tsps. double-acting baking powder
¼ cup sugar
1 tsp. salt
¼ cup butter or margarine

3 eggs, well beaten
1 cup milk
1 cup golden seedless raisins
½ cup Welch® Concord Grape Jelly

In a bowl, sift together flour, baking powder, sugar and salt. Cut in butter. Mix eggs, milk and raisins; blend into flour mixture. Stir lightly just to dampen flour. (If too dry, add few drops more milk.) Spoon into greased muffin-pan cups. Push 1 spoonful of grape jelly down into batter of each cup. Bake in a preheated hot oven (425°F.) approximately 20 minutes or until done. Serve hot. Makes 12.

7.

Apple Pie and
Other Americana

After traveling through many other countries, I've come to the conclusion that America is the only place you'll find real honest-to-goodness pie. In London when I asked for apple pie in a very good restaurant I was served stewed apples, watery and insufficiently sugared, under a tough, dry crust. The same could be said of all the British fruit pies I sampled. They don't even call pies by that name there—they call them tarts! The many delectable pies familiar to even the least knowledgeable cook in this country have never been heard of over there. Incredible, but true.

In France there are even fewer pies than in Great Britain. The only real pie I had in all of Paris was a delicious seafood pie which was served to me at the elegant Ritz Hotel. But one seafood pie does not, cannot, make a "pie-ish" nation; and the little delectable tarts heaped with fruit which the French patisseries offer have as much relation to a magnificent Southern Chocolate or fresh coconut pie as a Basque beret has to a western ten-gallon hat.

In Spain pie is unknown. So now we have the real reason for the voyage of Columbus. In Italy I was served what was called a pie, but it was much closer to a very fancy cake, decked with white icing and decorated with scrolls and sprays and dots and dashes of pink and green. Any intelligent New England pumpkin pie would have laughed itself to a custard at the idea of calling this a pie.

No, pie is America's own. There are, to be sure, desserts of equal stature in many other parts of the world; but pie, the real thing, is unique to this country.

It's hard to imagine anything better to eat than the old-fashioned two-crust Rosy Apple Pie that leads off this chapter, unless it's the Deep-Dish Apple Pie with its airy, light, puff pastry topping that follows or the Love Apple Pie that comes after that, served warm with a dollop of vanilla ice cream. But then you are going to love all of the pies in this chapter. Each one is an "asked-for" favorite featured by a top food company on their label or in advertising. They are indeed extra special. As long as you have a decent oven, each one is a snap to prepare. When you consider how good they taste and what a pretty picture they make when served, you will agree that they are well worth the small effort it takes to make them.

Rosy Apple Pie

Apple pie is America's own. Years of intensive baking by ardent cooks have given it its present shape, infinite variety, goodness and overwhelming popularity. This one, with a pinky amber, sweet tart filling was created by the cooks at the Crisco® test kitchens. You'll love it, as have almost a million other lovers of great apple pie.

Crisco® Oil Pie Crust
(For 9-inch double crust)

2⅔ cups sifted all purpose enriched flour
  1 teaspoon salt
  ¾ cup Crisco® Oil
  ¼ cup water

Mix flour and salt in a bowl. Add Crisco® Oil and water. Stir with a fork until blended and dough holds together. Divide in half and form to flat circles.

Roll out half the dough between two squares of waxed paper until circle of dough touches edges of paper. Dampen working surface to prevent waxed paper from slipping as dough is rolled.

Peel off top paper. Pick up rolled dough with bottom paper and turn onto pie plate, paper side up. Carefully peel off paper and press dough into pie plate. Trim dough even with edge of plate.

Roll remaining dough in the same way for the top crust. Add filling to pastry-lined pie plate. Peel waxed paper from top crust and place over filling. Trim about ½ inch beyond edge of pie plate. Fold edge of top crust under edge of bottom crust. Seal by fluting with fingers or fork. Prick or slit top crust to allow for escape of steam. Bake as directed under filling recipe.

Rosy Apple Filling

¾ cup sugar
½ cup water
¼ cup red cinnamon
   candies (red hots)
5 medium cooking apples
   (about 5 cups apple slices)
1 Tbs. flour
1 tsp. lemon juice
1 Tbs. butter or margarine

In a medium saucepan combine sugar, water and cinnamon candies; cook until candies dissolve. Pare, core, and slice apples; add to sugar mixture; simmer until apples are red. Drain; save syrup. Blend flour into cooled syrup and add lemon juice. Spread apples in a pastry-lined 9-inch pie plate; pour syrup over apples. Dot with butter. Cover with top crust; seal and flute edges. Cut slits for escape of steam. Bake at 400°F. about 30 minutes, until desired brownness. Makes 1 pie.

Deep-Dish Apple Pie

A simply beautiful and extra-festive pie. A sensation ever since it first appeared in 1970 on the Pepperidge Farm® Frozen Patty Shell package.

2 1-lb. 4-oz. cans apple pie
   filling
2 Tbs. grated orange rind
1 tsp. grated lemon rind

1 10-oz. package frozen patty
   shells, thawed
1 egg yolk
1 Tbs. water

Combine apple pie filling, orange rind and grated lemon rind. Pour into 1½-quart deep pie plate. Press the patty shells together. Roll out to make a circle ½ inch larger than top of pie plate. Trim off a ½-inch margin and fit this onto edge of pie crust on top of pastry rim on dish. Press lightly to seal. Trim off any surplus pastry. Crimp edges. Brush top with egg yolk mixed with water. Fashion shapes from pastry trimmings and use to decorate the crust. Brush the trimmings with the egg yolk and water mixture. Bake at 450°F. for 20 to 25 minutes.

Love Apple Pie

Love this Love Apple Pie. It's a Heinz® Tomato Ketchup classic recipe chosen from their 100 all-time top favorites. You don't really taste the ketchup but it gives this pie an intriguing sweet/tart taste.

⅓ cup Heinz® Tomato Ketchup
2 tsps. lemon juice
5 cups thinly sliced, pared cooking apples
¾ cup granulated sugar
¾ cup all-purpose flour
½ tsp. ground cinnamon
⅓ cup butter or margarine, softened
1 unbaked 9-inch pie shell

Blend Ketchup and lemon juice;* combine with apples. Combine sugar, flour and cinnamon; cut in butter until thoroughly mixed. Fill pie shell with apples; top with sugar mixture. Bake in 375°F. oven, 40 to 45 minutes or until apples are cooked. Serve warm with vanilla ice cream, if desired. Makes one 9-inch pie.

* If apples are very tart, add 1 to 2 Tbs. sugar to Ketchup mixture.

Cherry Cheese Pie

Cherry Cheese Pie is probably today's most popular recipe using Eagle® Brand Sweetened Condensed Milk and the one requested most by people. It appeared almost 20 years ago as Cherry-O Cream Cheese Pie in a recipe booklet and since has been on the can label and in advertisements. A similar recipe, however, was part of the first Eagle® Brand cookbook done in 1919.

1 9-inch graham cracker crumb crust
1 8-oz. package cream cheese, softened
1 14-oz. can Eagle® Brand Sweetened Condensed Milk (*not* evaporated milk)
⅓ cup ReaLemon® Reconstituted Lemon Juice
Canned cherry pie filling, chilled
Ambrosia Topping (below) or Cherry Nut Topping (below)

In large mixer bowl, beat cheese until fluffy. Beat in Eagle® Brand until smooth. Stir in ReaLemon® and vanilla. Pour into crust. Chill 3 hours or until set. Top with desired amount of pie filling before serving. Refrigerate leftovers. Makes one 9-inch pie.

Ambrosia Topping

½ cup peach or apricot preserves
¼ cup flaked coconut
2 Tbs. orange-flavored liqueur
2 tsps. corn starch
fresh orange sections (1 or 2 oranges)

In small saucepan, combine first four ingredients. Cook and stir until thickened. Remove from heat. Chill thoroughly. Spread over pie; arrange orange sections over top.

Cranberry Nut Topping

1 cup chilled cranberry-orange relish
½ cup chopped walnuts
1 tsp. grated orange rind

In small bowl, combine relish, walnuts and orange rind. Spread over pie. Garnish with orange twists, if desired.

No-Bake Pumpkin Pie

In 1931, the Borden® Company offered cooks $25 for new recipes made with Eagle® Brand Sweetened Condensed Milk. All of 80,000 recipes were read and graded and of those, 1,000 new recipes were tested in the kitchens. No-Bake Pumpkin Pie was among those selected and included in a booklet called "The Most Amazing Short-Cuts in Cooking You Ever Heard Of." It's still one of the most popular in their all-time favorites file.

1 envelope Knox®
  Unflavored Gelatine
1 tsp. ground cinnamon
½ tsp. ground ginger
½ tsp. ground nutmeg
½ tsp. salt
1 14-oz. can Eagle® Brand
  Sweetened Condensed
  Milk (*not* evaporated milk)

2 eggs, well beaten
1 16-oz. can pumpkin
  (about 2 cups)
1 graham cracker or butter
  flavored Ready® Crust pie
  crust

In heavy medium saucepan, combine unflavored gelatine, cinnamon, ginger, nutmeg and salt; stir in Sweetened Condensed Milk and eggs. Mix well. Let stand 1 minute. Over *low* heat, cook and stir constantly until gelatine dissolves and mixture thickens slightly, about 10 minutes. Remove from heat. Stir in pumpkin; mix well. Pour into prepared crust. Chill 3 hours or until set. Garnish as desired. Refrigerate leftovers.

Walnut Meringue Pie

This wonderful confection was first made for me by my Aunt Sally in Shreveport, Louisiana. It's a perfect dessert for special occasions; a luscious creation from Pet Ritz® that truly looks like a celebration. Tastes like one too!

3 egg whites, room temperature	20 Ritz Crackers, broken in fourths
¼ tsp. salt	4 cups cut-up fresh fruits in season, or canned, very well-drained
½ tsp. baking powder	
1 cup granulated sugar	
1 tsp. vanilla extract	½ cup heavy cream, whipped, unsweetened
⅔ cup broken walnuts	

Beat egg whites until soft peaks form. Add salt and baking powder. Gradually beat in sugar; continue beating until stiff and glossy. Add vanilla extract. Lightly fold in next two ingredients. Spread mixture over bottom and sides of well-greased pie plate. Build up sides. Bake in a preheated slow oven (325°F.) 25 to 30 minutes. Cool completely on wire rack. Just before serving, fill center with fruit. Serve cream separately. Makes 8 (3½-inch) wedges.

Southern Sweet Chocolate Pie

Most men adore chocolate pie—but I know one New York food editor whose favorite is not just chocolate but Southern chocolate pie. As he spent his childhood in the deep South, it's no wonder and I must admit this recipe that he sent me has a unique flavor unbuyable at any bakery. Baker's® German Sweet Chocolate gets the credit.

1 4-oz. package Baker's®	3 eggs
German Sweet	1 tsp. vanilla
Chocolate	1 unbaked 9-inch pie shell,
¼ cup butter or margarine	with high-fluted rim*
1 13-oz. can evaporated	1⅓ cups (about) Baker's®
milk	Angel Flake Coconut
1 cup sugar	½ cup chopped pecans

Heat Chocolate with butter in saucepan over low heat, stirring until melted and smooth. Remove from heat; gradually blend in evaporated milk and sugar. Beat in eggs and vanilla. Gradually blend in chocolate mixture. Pour into pie shell; sprinkle with coconut and nuts. (Shell will be quite full, but filling will not rise over sides.) Bake at 375°F. for 45 to 50 minutes, or until top is puffed and browned. (Filling will be soft, but will set while cooling.) Cool at least 4 hours.

Note: If topping browns too quickly, cover loosely with aluminum foil during the last 15 minutes of baking. Pie may be wrapped and stored in freezer; thaw before serving.

* Or Use 2 unbaked 8-inch pie shells, baked about 45 minutes.

Coconut Pear Pie Supreme

Part of the popularity of this luxurious dessert is its ease of preparation, but it is the rich and elegant taste that has made it one of the top ten best recipes in the Holland House® test kitchen as well as with its consumers.

1 fully baked 8- or 9-inch
  pie shell
1 15-oz. container whole
  milk Ricotta cheese
¾ cup Coco Casa® Cream of
  Coconut
1 Tbs. candied fruit

1 Tbs. mini chocolate bits
6 to 8 pear halves,
  stewed or canned
  Apricot glaze, warmed
  Bitter chocolate curls or
  rounds for garnish

Whip Ricotta cheese until smooth and glossy. Add
Cream of Coconut and mix well. Fold in candied fruit
and chocolate bits. Refrigerate for 3 hours or overnight.
Spread Ricotta filling evenly into pie shell. Place drained
pears in an attractive pattern over filling and brush with
apricot glaze. Decorate with curls or rounds of chocolate.

Orange Ambrosia Pie

**There's always a reason when a recipe becomes a "top favo-
rite" and "an all-time great." I think it's the contrast of the
fresh orange filling to this crunchy crust that makes this one
such a heavenly hit.**

3 to 4 oranges, peeled and
  cut into small pieces (2½
  cups)
½ cup and ⅓ cup sugar
1 cup orange juice
  (approximately)
3 tablespoons corn starch

1 3 oz. package cream
  cheese, softened
¼ teaspoon ground ginger
1 tablespoon milk
¼ to ½ cup flaked coconut
  Chex® Crust (below)

To prepare Filling, mix orange pieces and ½ cup sugar.
Set aside while preparing Chex Crust (below). Then
continue with Filling: Drain syrup from oranges. Add
enough orange juice to make 1½ cups. In medium-size
saucepan combine corn starch and remaining ⅓ cup
sugar. Add orange juice. Cook and stir over medium

heat until very thick and clear. Cool to lukewarm. Combine cream cheese, ginger and milk. Spread on bottom and sides of crust. Stir orange pieces into sauce. Turn into crust. Sprinkle with coconut. Chill at least two hours or until sauce is set. For easy serving, set pie plate in warm water for 1 minute before cutting.

Chex® Crust

4 cups Rice Chex® Cereal® crushed to 1 cup
¼ cup packed brown sugar
¼ tsp. ground ginger
⅓ cup butter or margarine, melted

Preheat oven to 300°F. Butter 9-inch pie plate. Combine Rice Chex® crumbs, sugar and ginger. Add butter. Mix thoroughly. Press evenly onto bottom and sides of pie plate. Bake 10 minutes. Cool completely.

Creamy Cheese Pie

Oh my, this is good! It's a snap, crackle and pop kind of recipe from the Kellogg's® people. You'll be smiled upon for preparing it, I assure you.

3 cups Kellogg's® Rice Krispies® cereal, crushed to measure 1½ cups
¼ cup sugar
½ tsp. ground cinnamon
½ cup margarine or butter, melted
4 3-oz. packages cream cheese, softened
2 eggs

1 tsp. vanilla flavoring
⅓ cup sugar
1 tsp. lemon juice
1 8-oz. carton (1 cup) dairy sour cream
2 Tbs. sugar
1 1-lb., 5-oz. can cherry pie filling
1 tsp. lemon juice

Combine crushed Rice Krispies® Cereal, ¼ cup sugar and cinnamon with the margarine. Press firmly in 9-inch pie pan to form crust. Set aside. In large mixing bowl, beat cream cheese until smooth. Add eggs, vanilla, ⅓ cup sugar and 1 teaspoon lemon juice, mixing until well combined. Pour mixture into crust. Bake in oven at 375°F. about 20 minutes, or until set. While pie is baking, stir together sour cream and 2 Tbs. sugar. Remove pie from oven. Spread sour cream mixture over top. Return to oven. Bake 5 minutes longer. Remove from oven. Cool. Stir together pie filling and the remaining 1 tsp. lemon juice. Spread over top of cooled pie. Chill. Makes 1 9-inch pie.

Fudge Sundae Pie

When this easy-to-prepare ice cream pie was featured in a series of national advertisements by Kellogg's®, it was an instant success. It's just plain delicious.

¼ cup corn syrup
2 Tbs. firmly packed brown sugar
3 Tbs. margarine or butter
2½ cups Kellogg's® Rice Krispies® Cereal

¼ cup peanut butter
¼ cup fudge sauce for ice cream
3 Tbs. corn syrup
1 quart vanilla ice cream

Combine ¼ cup corn syrup, brown sugar and margarine in medium-size saucepan. Cook over low heat, stirring occasionally, until mixture begins to boil. Remove from heat. Add Rice Krispies® Cereal, stirring until well coated. Press evenly in 9-inch pie pan to form crust. Stir together peanut butter, fudge sauce and the corn syrup. Spread half the peanut butter mixture over crust. Freeze until firm. Allow ice cream to soften slightly. Spoon into frozen pie crust, spreading evenly. Freeze until firm. Let pie stand at room temperature about 10 minutes before cutting. Warm remaining peanut butter mixture and drizzle over top. Makes 8 servings.

Frosty Mint Ice Cream Pies

These deliciously different pies are from a special *Pillsbury*® *Plus Cookbook*. The crust puffs during baking and then collapses to form the pie shell shape. A beautiful dessert.

Pie Shells

1 package Pillsbury® Plus Chocolate Mint,
   Devil's Food or Dark Chocolate Cake
   Mix
¾ cup Pillsbury® Ready To Spread
   Chocolate Fudge Frosting Supreme
¾ cup water
¼ cup oil

Filling

6 cups (1¼ quarts) mint chocolate chip
   or your favorite ice cream, softened

Heat oven to 350°F. Generously grease bottom, sides and rim of two 9-inch pie pans or round cake pans.* In large bowl, blend all shell ingredients at low speed until moistened; beat 2 minutes at highest speed. Spread half of

* Do not use 8-inch pie or cake pans.

batter (2¼ cups) in bottom of each pan. Do not spread up sides of pan. Bake at 350°F. for 25 to 30 minutes; *Do not overbake*. Cakes will collapse to form shells. Cool completely. In large bowl, blend ice cream until smooth; spread evenly in center of each shell leaving a ½-inch rim. If desired, heat remaining frosting just until softened. Drop by spoonfuls on top of ice cream and swirl with knife. Freeze at least 2 hours. Store in freezer. Wrap frozen pies airtight to avoid freezer burn. Makes 2 pies, 12 servings.

Fresh Coconut Cream Pie

Now here's a pie for you; a real "coconutty" coconut pie. It's from the inside label of the Holland House® Cream of Coconut can. They tell me at Holland House® that this is the recipe that makes over a half-million people buy their second and third can of this lovely liquid.

1 10-inch baked pie shell
6 ozs. Coco Casa® Cream of Coconut
¼ cup milk
10 ozs. mini-marshmallows

3 cups heavy cream, whipped stiff
2 cups coconut flakes (fresh or canned)

Mix Cream of Coconut with milk. Add marshmallows. Cook over low heat until marshmallows melt. Cool in bowl and refrigerate 1 hour or until mixture starts to jell. Beat jelled mixture with electric mixer until frothy. Carefully, fold in whipped cream. Blend in 1 cup flaked coconut, by hand. Pour into baked pie shell. Sprinkle remaining cup of flaked coconut (toast if desired) over pie and refrigerate at least 6 hours before serving. Makes 1 10-inch pie.

Vanilla Nut Crumb Crust

Here's the accurate and predictable, as well as delectable, nut crumb pie crust that you and just about every good cook has asked for.

1 cup finely crushed vanilla wafers (about 29)

½ cup Planters® Pecan Pieces, Planters® Walnut Pieces, Planters® Blanched Almonds or Planters® Salted Peanuts, ground

⅓ cup Blue Bonnet® Margarine, melted*

In a small bowl, combine vanilla wafer crumbs, ground Planters® nuts and Blue Bonnet® Margarine. Press mixture against sides and bottom of a 9-inch pie plate. Bake at 375°F. for 7 to 8 minutes, or until lightly browned. Cool. Fill as desired.

Chocolate Variation: Use 1 cup finely crushed chocolate wafers (about 17) in place of vanilla wafers.

* If Planters® Salted Peanuts are used increase margarine to 6 Tbs.

Peach Gem Pie

This lovely pie from the Jell-O® kitchens has inspired more than a few people to try their hand at pie making, and with good reason; it's a snap to make and just about any fresh or canned fruit may be substituted for the peaches. Try strawberry Jello® and chopped fresh strawberries or lime Jello® with blueberries—or, try your own ideas.

1 3-oz. package Jell-O®
Orange Gelatin
1 cup boiling water
2 cups ice cubes
½ tsp. almond extract

2 cups sliced peeled fresh
peaches*
1 baked 9-inch pie shell,
cooled

Dissolve gelatin in boiling water. Add ice cubes and stir constantly until gelatin starts to thicken—3 to 5 minutes. Remove any unmelted ice. Add almond extract and peaches. Pour into pie shell. Chill until firm—about 3 hours. Garnish with whipped topping and toasted almonds, if desired. Makes 1 9-inch pie.

* Or use 1 16-oz. can sliced peaches, drained

Coffee Yogurt Chiffon Pie

At your insistence, here's "a" famous Dannon® Yogurt Pie. I must admit it's really delicious.

Crumb crust
1⅓ cups chocolate wafer crumbs
3 Tbs. butter or margarine, melted

Combine cookie crumbs and butter. Reserve 3 Tbs. of crumbs for top of pie and press remaining crumbs on bottom and sides of 9-inch pie plate.·

Filling
1 envelope Knox®
Unflavored Gelatine
⅔ cup sugar, divided
3 eggs, separated
¾ cup milk
1 8-oz. container Dannon®
Coffee Yogurt

Mix Gelatine and ⅓ cup sugar in saucepan. Beat egg yolks and milk together and stir into Gelatine mixture. Cook, stirring constantly over low heat for 4 or 5 minutes, until gelatine dissolves and mixture thickens slightly. Cool slightly and blend in yogurt. Chill, stirring occasionally, until mixture mounds slightly when dropped from a spoon. Beat egg whites until soft peaks form. Gradually beat in remaining ⅓ cup sugar, beat until stiff. Fold into Gelatine mixture. Turn into prepared pie shell and chill until firm. Garnish with reserved cookie crumbs. Makes 1 9-inch pie.

Planters® Nut Crust

A perfected all-nut crust that is constantly requested.

2 cups Planters® Salted
  Peanuts, Planters®
  Walnuts, Planters® Pecan
  Pieces, or Planters®
  Blanched Almonds,
  ground

3 Tbs. Blue Bonnet®
  Margarine, melted*
1 Tbs. sugar

Combine ground Nuts, Blue Bonnet® Margarine and sugar. Press evenly into bottom and on sides of 9-inch pie plate. Bake at 350°F. for 10 to 12 minutes. Cool and fill as desired.

* Increase to 4 Tbs. margarine for walnut or pecan crust.

Nutty Meringue Pie Shell

The other most requested pie shell from Planters®. It's angels' food, no less.

3 egg whites (at room temperature)
¼ tsp. cream of tartar
⅛ tsp. salt
¾ cup sugar
½ tsp. vanilla extract

¼ cup Planters® Pecan Pieces, Planters® Walnuts, Planters® Blanched Almonds, or Planters® Salted Peanuts, coarsely chopped

Combine egg whites, cream of tartar and salt in small bowl of electric mixer. Beat on high speed until soft peaks form. Gradually add sugar, beating until stiff peaks form. Mix in vanilla. Spread meringue evenly over bottom and sides of a greased and floured 9-inch pie plate. Sprinkle Planters® Nuts over meringue in bottom of shell. Bake at 300°F. for 40 to 45 minutes, or until lightly browned. Cool. Fill as desired.

Foolproof Meringue

Terrific, just terrific. The enthusiasm for this recipe has been going strong since Kraft® developed it some 15 years ago.

3 egg whites
  Dash of salt
1 cup (½ of 7-oz. jar) Kraft® Marshmallow Creme

Beat egg whites and salt until soft peaks form. Gradually add marshmallow creme, beating until stiff peaks form. Spread over pie filling, sealing to edge of crust. Bake at 350°F. 12 to 15 minutes or until lightly browned. Cool.

8.

The Best-I-Ever-Ate Cakes and Other Fabulous Desserts

You know the world is filled with many good things, but the "best," well now that's a bit more rare. For instance, plain baked apples are certainly good, as I'm sure you know. However, "Butter-Cream Apples"—apples baked with butter and sugar that turns to a rich sauce when cream is added—are something else entirely and much better. Just as a spice cake made moist and rich with fresh apples and served with a brandy hard sauce is better than plain.

I've filled this chapter with recipes for cakes and desserts that are all better than good. In fact, they are the best I ever ate. Scrumptious, old-fashioned strawberry shortcake (the real thing), delicate and delectable jelly roll, Almond Candy Cake—light as a cloud and a veritable Viennese Opera of sweet flavors—are only the beginning.

I've gone through the permanent files at the test kitchens of our top food companies and pulled out what really are the best recipes for cakes and desserts of their kind. A classic French mousse, made particularly sensational with coffee liqueur, a raisin cake that can only be called amazing, it's that good, Frosty Orange Stars—star-shaped orange shells filled with fruited ice cream (the most beautiful frozen dessert you ever have seen), and scores of others. Each one is so easy to prepare, so fail-proof, you just can't lose, even if your skills at dessert-making have been limited to defrosting "store bought."

I put these recipes in a class with fine wine and rare spices—among the luxury items of the food world. To my way of thinking they should be dealt with accordingly. While it's fine to be thrifty and frugal when you're planning your over-all budget or shopping for staples, when you're making a fine dessert, it's best to go all out and dismiss, just this once, all thought of time and expense. Forget calories, too, and treat yourself and everyone else to a fair share of the best.

Old-Fashioned Jelly Roll

How long since you've had a slice of homemade jelly roll cake? Too long I'll bet. If your mother didn't save her recipe, here it is, just as printed on the Welch® Concord Grape Jelly jar over 15 years ago.

4 eggs
¾ cup sifted all-purpose or
  cake flour
1 tsp. baking powder
¼ tsp. salt
¾ cup sugar

1 tsp. vanilla extract or
  1 Tbs. grated orange
  peel
Confectioners sugar
1 10-oz. jar Welch's®
  Concord Grape Jelly

In electric mixer bowl, let eggs warm to room temperature (about 1 hour). Sift together flour, baking powder and salt; set aside. At high speed, beat eggs until thick and lemon colored. Gradually beat in sugar, 2 Tbs. at a time, continuing to beat until very thick and light (about 5 minutes). At low speed, blend in sifted dry ingredients and vanilla just until combined. Spread evenly in a jelly-roll pan, 15 × 10½ × 1 inches, lined with greased wax paper. Bake in a preheated hot oven (400°F.) until surface springs back when gently pressed with fingertip (about 10 to 13 minutes). Sift confectioners sugar on a clean towel in a 15 × 10-inch oblong. With sharp knife, loosen sides of cake from pan. Turn onto the sugared towel; gently peel off wax paper and trim off crisp edges. Starting with 10-inch side, roll cake in towel; place seam side down on wire rack until cool. Gently unroll cake, remove towel and spread with jelly (beaten with fork to spreading consistency). Reroll and place seam side down, on serving plate; cover loosely with foil. Chill at least 1 hour. Serve topped with sifted confectioners sugar. Serves 10.

Golden Beauty Prune Cake

**A half-century of good cooks have baked this Sunsweet®
Prune Cake. It's as moist, rich and delicious today as it was
50 years ago.**

1 cup snipped cooked
   Sunsweet® Prunes
½ cup butter or margarine
1 cup granulated sugar
½ cup brown sugar,
   packed
1 tsp. vanilla
2 large eggs, beaten
2½ cups sifted all-purpose
   flour

¾ tsp. baking powder
¾ tsp. baking soda
¾ tsp. salt
½ tsp. cinnamon
¼ tsp. nutmeg
¼ tsp. cloves
1 cup buttermilk
   Mocha Frosting (below)

Cook prunes by package directions; drain and snip.
Cream butter with sugars and vanilla until light and
fluffy. Beat in eggs. (Mixture may appear slightly curdled.) Resift flour with baking powder, soda, salt and
spices. Blend into creamed mixture alternately with buttermilk, beginning and ending with flour mixture. Fold in
prunes. Turn into 2 well greased, 8-inch layer cake pans.
Bake in oven center at 375°F. for about 30 minutes, until
cakes test done. Remove from oven; let stand 10 minutes,
then turn out onto wire racks to cool. When cold, spread
Mocha Frosting between layers and on top and sides of
cake. Makes 1 8-inch cake.

Mocha Frosting

1 tsp. instant coffee powder
¼ cup milk
⅓ cup soft butter or margarine
1 lb. powdered sugar, sifted.

Dissolve coffee powder in milk. Combine with butter or margarine and powdered sugar. Beat until smooth, adding a few drops more milk if needed for good spreading consistency.

Famous Chocolate Wafer Roll

Here is another of those "too good to take off the package" recipes. Ridiculously easy to make, fabulously rich-tasting and positively exotic when sliced and served. It's the Famous Chocolate Wafers® that have made this a famous American classic dessert.

1 cup heavy cream
¼ cup confectioners sugar
½ tsp. vanilla extract
20 Famous Chocolate Wafers®

Whip cream with sugar and vanilla, until stiff. Reserve 1 cup. Spread Famous Chocolate Wafers® with remaining cream and arrange in stacks of 4 or 5. Chill 15 minutes. Lay stacks on edge to make one long roll. Spread remaining cream on outside of roll. Chill 3 to 4 hours, or overnight, covered. To serve, cut diagonally.

Makes 8 ¾-inch slices.

Variation: Substitute 1 Tbs. instant coffee for vanilla extract, and garnish with chocolate curls.

Deluxe Shortcake

No true American cookbook would be complete without a real shortcake made with your own, not-too-sweet, biscuit-like layers, not with "store-bought" sponge cake.

2 cups Pillsbury's® Best Self-Rising or Unbleached Self-Rising Flour
2 Tbs. sugar
½ cup shortening
¾ cup half-and-half or whipping cream
2 Tbs. margarine or butter, melted
1 Tbs. sugar
1 cup whipping cream, whipped
6 cups sliced strawberries or other favorite fruit

Heat oven to 425°F. Lightly spoon flour into measuring cup; level off. In large bowl, combine flour and sugar. Cut shortening into flour mixture with fork until consistency of coarse meal. Add half-and-half to flour mixture; stir just until moistened. Spread batter in 2 ungreased 8-inch round pans. Brush melted margarine over batter; sprinkle with sugar. Bake at 425°F. for 12 to 18 minutes or until light golden brown. Immediately remove from pans; cool completely. Fill and top layers with whipped cream and strawberries. Refrigerate leftovers. Makes 12 servings.

Old-Fashioned Cocoa Mint Cake

Memories were soon made when this "pepperminty-chocolatey" recipe was first printed in Hershey's® 1930 cookbook.

⅔ cup butter
1⅔ cups granulated sugar
3 eggs
2 cups all-purpose flour
⅔ cup Hershey's® Cocoa
1¼ tsps. baking soda
¼ tsp. baking powder

1 tsp. salt
1⅓ cups milk
½ cup crushed peppermint candy
Cocoa Peppermint Icing (below)

Cream butter, sugar and eggs until fluffy, and beat vigorously 3 minutes (high speed of mixer). Combine flour, cocoa, baking soda, baking powder and salt; add alternately with milk to creamed mixture. Blend in crushed candy. Pour batter into 2 greased and floured 9-inch cake pans. Bake in a moderate oven (350°) for 35 minutes. Cool 10 minutes before removing from pans. Ice cake with Cocoa Peppermint Icing.

Cocoa Peppermint Icing

½ cup butter
½ cup Hershey's® Cocoa
3⅔ cups (1-lb. box) confectioners sugar

7 Tbs. milk
1 tsp. vanilla
1 Tbs. crushed peppermint candy

Melt the butter in a saucepan; add the Cocoa and heat 1 minute or until smooth, stirring constantly. Alternately add sugar and milk, beating to spreading consistency. Blend in vanilla and peppermint candy. Makes about 2¼ cups icing or enough for an 8- or 9-inch layer cake.

Holiday Gift Cake

On the label of Philadelphia® Brand Cream Cheese a long time ago, but still a much-requested recipe.

1 8-oz. package
Philadelphia® Brand
Cream Cheese
1 cup Parkay® Margarine
1½ cups sugar
1½ tsps. vanilla
4 eggs
2¼ cups sifted cake flour
1½ tsps. baking powder

¾ cup well-drained
chopped Maraschino
cherries
½ cup chopped pecans
½ cup finely chopped
pecans
1½ cups sifted confectioners
sugar
2 Tbs. milk

Combine softened cream cheese, margarine, sugar and vanilla, mixing until well blended. Add eggs, one at a time, mixing well after each addition. Gradually add 2 cups flour sifted with baking powder, mixing well after each addition. Toss remaining flour with cherries and chopped nuts; fold into batter. Grease a 10-inch Bundt or tube pan; sprinkle with finely chopped nuts. Pour batter into pan; bake at 325°F. 1 hour and 20 minutes. Cool 5 minutes; remove from pan. Cool thoroughly. Glaze with mixture of confectioners sugar and milk. Garnish with cherries and nuts, if desired. Makes 1 cake.

Chocolate Upside-Down Cake

In the 1940's when upside-down cakes were at their height of popularity, this one rated four stars. They tell me at the Hershey® test kitchens it has been rediscovered, and requests for the recipe have doubled in the last few years. No wonder; it is *good!*

3 Tbs. butter, melted
½ cup light brown sugar, packed
2 Tbs. light corn syrup
1 29-oz. can sliced peaches or pear halves, well drained
Maraschino cherries, halved
½ cup chopped nuts (optional)

½ cup butter or margarine
1¼ cups sugar
2 eggs
1 tsp. vanilla
1¼ cups unsifted all-purpose flour
⅓ cup Hershey's® Cocoa
¾ tsp. baking soda
½ tsp. salt
⅔ cup buttermilk or sour milk*

Combine 3 Tbs. butter, brown sugar and corn syrup in bottom of a 12-cup Bundt pan or 10-inch tube pan. (Do not use a removable-bottom tube pan.) Arrange sliced peaches or pear halves and cherries in a decorative design. Sprinkle with nuts. Cream ½ cup butter and sugar until light and fluffy. Add eggs, one at a time, beating well after each addition; add vanilla. Combine flour, cocoa, baking soda and salt; add to creamed mixture alternately with buttermilk. Pour batter evenly over fruit and nuts in pan. Bake at 350°F. for 40 to 45 minutes for Bundt pan, 50 to 55 minutes for tube pan or until cake tester inserted in center comes out clean. Immediately invert onto serving plate; leave pan over cake a few minutes. Serve warm with sweetened whipped cream if desired.

* To Sour Milk: Use 2 tsps. vinegar plus milk to equal ⅔ cup.

Amazin' Raisin Cake

The name fits; a rather terrific cake. When it appeared in a national ad the response from consumers was, in a word, amazing.

3 cups unsifted flour
2 cups sugar
1 cup Hellmann's® Best Foods Real Mayonnaise
⅓ cup milk
2 eggs
2 tsps. baking soda
1½ tsps. ground cinnamon
½ tsp. ground nutmeg
½ tsp. salt
¼ tsp. ground cloves
3 cups chopped peeled apples
1 cup seedless raisins
1 cup coarsely chopped walnuts
2 cups whipped cream

Grease and flour 2 9-inch round baking pans. In large bowl with mixer at low speed, scraping bowl frequently, beat together flour, sugar, Real Mayonnaise, milk, eggs, baking soda, cinnamon, nutmeg, salt and cloves 2 minutes or beat vigorously 300 strokes by hand. (Batter will be thick.) With spoon stir in apples, raisins and nuts. Spoon into prepared pans. Bake in 350°F. oven 45 minutes or until cake tester inserted in center comes out clean. Cool in pans on wire racks 10 minutes. Remove and cool on wire racks. Fill and frost with whipped cream. Makes 8 servings.

Amaretto Raisin Bundt Cake

This cake is a positive triumph. It is a party cake for sure. Thousands have written in for copies of this recipe since it appeared only a few short years ago in a national magazine advertisement for Hiram Walker® Amaretto.

1 package Pillsbury® Pound Cake Supreme Bundt Cake Mix
½ cup dairy sour cream
¼ cup margarine or butter, softened
½ cup water
⅓ cup Hiram Walker® Amaretto
3 eggs
2 cups (1 lb.) candied fruit mixture
1 cup Sun-Maid® Raisins
1 cup chopped nuts
Sauce (below)

Heat oven to 325°F. Grease 12-cup Bundt pan. In large bowl, combine two clear packets of Cake Mix and remaining cake ingredients, except fruit, raisins and nuts. Blend until moistened; beat 2 minutes at medium speed. Fold in fruit, raisins and nuts. Pour into pan. Bake at 325°F. for 70 to 80 minutes until toothpick inserted in center comes out clean. *Cool upright* in pan on rack 25 minutes; invert onto plate. Cool completely. Sprinkle or sift topping packet over top of cake. Makes 16 servings.

Sauce

1½ cups sugar	¼ cup Hiram Walker® Amaretto
4 Tbs. corn starch	2 Tbs. lemon juice
1½ cups water	½ cup Sun-Maid® Raisins
4 Tbs. margarine or butter	

To prepare sauce, mix sugar and corn starch in saucepan. Gradually stir in water. Over medium heat stirring constantly, heat to boiling; boil 1 minute. Remove from heat; stir in margarine, Amaretto, juice and raisins. Serve warm over cooled cake.

Carrot Cake

A "top-request" recipe and a particular favorite at the Betty Crocker® test kitchens. Made to order for mid-morning coffee, afternoon tea or after-school milk.

2 cups Bisquick® Baking Mix	1½ cups shredded carrots
½ cup packed brown sugar	⅓ cup vegetable oil
½ cup chopped nuts	3 eggs
2 tsps. ground cinnamon	¼ cup chopped nuts
1 tsp. ground nutmeg	Cream Cheese Frosting (below)

Heat oven to 350°F. Grease and flour square pan, 9 × 9 × 2 inches. Beat all ingredients except frosting and ¼ c. nuts on low speed, scraping bowl constantly, 30 seconds. Beat on medium speed, scraping bowl occasionally, 2 minutes. Pour into pan. Bake until wooden pick inserted in center comes out clean, about 30 minutes. Cool; frost with Cream Cheese Frosting. Sprinkle with nuts. Refrigerate any remaining cake.

Cream Cheese Frosting

1 3-oz. package cream cheese, softened
2 cups powdered sugar
1 Tbs. margarine or butter, softened
2 to 3 tsps. milk

Mix all ingredients until texture is smooth.

Cheese Cake Almondine

One of the simplest of all cheese cakes to make, it won a popularity contest back in the 1950's because of its sensational richness and flavor, from Planters®.

1½ cups finely crushed
    vanilla wafer crumbs
1¼ cups sugar
½ cup chopped Planters®
    Pecans
½ tsp. grated lemon rind
¼ cup Blue Bonnet®
    Margarine, melted
3 8-oz. packages cream
    cheese, softened

3 eggs
⅔ cup chopped Planters®
    Blanched Almonds
¾ tsp. almond extract
1 cup dairy sour cream
⅓ cup Planters® Sliced
    Almonds

Combine vanilla wafer crumbs, 2 Tbs. sugar, Planters® Pecans and lemon rind. Add melted Blue Bonnet® Margarine. Combine well and press mixture into the bottom of a lightly greased 8-inch spring-form pan. Refrigerate. Cream the cheese and 1 cup of the remaining sugar in large bowl until light and fluffy. Add eggs, one at a time, beating well after each addition. Blend in Planters® Blanched Almonds and ½ teaspoon almond extract. Pour into chilled crust. Bake at 375°F. for 45 minutes. Cool at room temperature for 30 minutes. Meanwhile, blend sour cream, remaining 2 Tbs. sugar and ¼ tsp. almond extract. Spread mixture over cooled cheese filling. Bake for an additional 10 minutes. Sprinkle with Planters® Sliced Almonds and cool. Refrigerate overnight before serving. Makes 1 cake.

Devil's Delight Cake

An old-fashioned honest-to-goodness Devil's Food Cake from Hershey's® 1934 Cookbook. This was always my choice for my own birthday, filled and lavishly covered with Creole Icing made with strong and clear black coffee.

4 squares Hershey's®
   Baking Chocolate, melted
⅔ cup brown sugar, packed
1 cup milk
1 egg yolk
⅓ cup butter
½ cup brown sugar, packed
2 egg yolks
2 cups sifted cake flour
¼ tsp. salt

1 tsp. baking soda
½ cup milk
1 tsp. vanilla
3 egg whites
½ cup brown sugar, packed
   Orange slices sprinkled
   with minced nutmeats
   and minced citron or
   candied ginger for
   garnishes

Combine melted baking chocolate with ⅔ cup brown sugar, 1 cup milk and 1 beaten egg yolk, and stir over simmering water until well blended. Cool slightly.

Cream butter, then add ½ cup brown sugar gradually, while beating constantly. Add 2 egg yolks well-beaten. Sift flour, salt and baking soda 3 times, and add to creamed mixture alternately with ½ cup milk, beating thoroughly. Add chocolate mixture and vanilla, and beat. Beat egg whites until foamy; gradually add ½ cup brown sugar and beat until stiff. Fold into batter. Pour into 2 buttered and floured 9-inch round cake pans. Bake in a moderate oven (350°F.) for 35 minutes. Spread layers and top with any favorite frosting, and garnish with orange slices, sprinkled with minced nutmeats and minced citron or candied ginger.

Creole Icing

     1 Tbs. softened butter
    ¼ cup clear black coffee
     3 Tbs. Hershey's® Cocoa
       Pinch of cinnamon
    3¼ cups confectioners sugar

Combine butter, coffee, Cocoa and cinnamon. Gradually add sugar, beating to spreading consistency. Makes 1½ cups icing or enough for an 8- or 9-inch layer cake.

Sun-Maid® Victory Cake

Sun-Maid® developed this easy-make cake back in the days of World War II. It's still one of their best.

1 cup Sun-Maid® Raisins	1 tsp. cloves
1 cup brown sugar (packed)	2 cups sifted all-purpose
1 cup water	flour
½ cup shortening	1 tsp. soda
1 tsp. cinnamon	½ tsp. salt
1 tsp. nutmeg	½ cup chopped walnuts

Combine Raisins, sugar, water, shortening and spices; heat to boiling and simmer 2 minutes. Cool 1 hour. Resift flour with soda and salt. Stir into raisin mixture, along with walnuts. Turn into greased 9-inch tube or square pan. Bake in slow oven (300°F.) 50 to 60 minutes, just until cake tests done. Cool in pan. Makes 1 9-inch cake.

Almond Candy Cake

One of the most popular cakes ever to appear in a national ad by the California Almond Growers Exchange.

1 large sponge or chiffon cake
  Filling (below)
  Maple Crisp topping (below)
1 cup toasted blanched almond halves

Split cake into 4 equal layers. Spread about half of Filling between cake layers. Spread remainder over top and sides of cake. Cover cake very thickly with Maple Crisp Topping, and stick almond halves porcupine fashion over top and sides of cake. Makes 16 to 20 servings.

Filling

2 cups whipping cream
2 Tbs. sugar
⅛ tsp. maple flavoring

Whip cream with sugar and flavoring.

Maple Crisp Topping

1½ cups sugar
⅓ cup water
¼ cup light corn syrup
1 Tbs. sifted baking soda
2 tsps. maple flavoring

Combine sugar, water and corn syrup in a saucepan, stirring until well blended. Boil over moderate heat to hard-crack stage (310°F.), until a small amount of syrup dropped into cold water will break with a brittle snap. Remove from heat, and stir in soda and maple flavoring. Stir vigorously until well blended, but not enough to destroy foam made by soda. Turn at once into ungreased shallow pan, about 9 inches square. Let stand without moving until completely cold. Knock out of pan and crush between sheets of waxed paper to make coarse crumbs.

Apple Spice Cake with Brandy Hard Sauce

Land O Lakes® Butter printed this scrumptious buttery spice cake recipe in an in-store recipe brochure. Serve it at your next dessert party and don't forget the coffee.

Cake

2 cups finely chopped apples	4 cups all-purpose flour
¼ cup water	4 tsp. baking soda
1½ cups Land O Lakes® Unsalted (Sweet) Butter, softened	2 tsp. *each* cinnamon and nutmeg
2 cups sugar	1 tsp. *each* salt and cloves
2 eggs	1 cup currants
	1 cup chopped pecans
	½ cup all-purpose flour

Hard Sauce

½ cup Land O Lakes® Unsalted (Sweet) Butter, softened
1 cup confectioners sugar
1 Tbs. brandy

Heat oven to 325°F. In 3-quart saucepan combine apples and water. Cook, uncovered, over medium heat, stirring occasionally, until apples are crisply tender (7 to 9 minutes). Remove from heat. Stir in butter until melted. Stir in sugar and eggs until well blended. In bowl combine 4 cups flour, baking soda, cinnamon, nutmeg, salt and cloves. Stir into apple mixture. In same bowl toss currants and pecans with ½ cup flour until coated. Stir into batter until well mixed. Spoon into 10-inch greased Bundt pan or tube pan. Bake in Bundt pan for 65 to 75 minutes (or tube pan for 70 to 80 minutes) until wooden pick inserted in center comes out clean. Cool in pan 15 minutes. Meanwhile, in 1½-quart mixer bowl combine all hard-sauce ingredients. Beat at medium speed until light and fluffy (3 to 5 minutes). Invert cake onto serving plate. Serve slices of warm cake with a dollop of 1 Tbs. hard sauce on each slice. Makes 1 10-inch cake with 1¼ cups hard sauce (20 servings).

Tip: If hard sauce is refrigerated, let stand at room temperature for 30 minutes before serving on warm cake.

Mince Meat Tarts

Mince meat pie is an American tradition, a holiday must. These tarts, from the people who bottle Angostura® Bitters, are lovely served just pleasantly warm from the oven, topped with chilled, lightly sweetened and brandied whipped cream.

1 14-oz. can pineapple chunks
1 9-oz. package mince meat
1 Tbs. Angostura®
2 packages pastry mix

Drain pineapple. Measure juice and add enough water to make 1½ cups. Slice chunks. Break up mince meat, add to liquid and simmer 2 minutes. Add pineapple. Cool and add Angostura®. Mix pastry according to directions on package. Roll one half of mixture at a time. Cut into 4-inch rounds. With small cutter, remove centers from half of the rounds. Arrange whole rounds on baking sheet and moisten edges. Place rounded Tbs. mince meat mixture in center of rounds, cover with pastry rings and press edges together. Bake in hot oven (450°F.) about 20 minutes until pastry is lightly browned. Makes 12 tarts.

Kahlua® Mousse

A dozen years ago Kahlua® introduced this fabulous version of a French classic. Prepare it for a special-occasion dinner party. It's a sensational dessert.

1 cup Kahlua®
¾ cup strong, brewed
   coffee
   Instant decaffeinated-
   coffee granules
1 cup confectioners sugar
¼ tsp. almond extract
1 envelope unflavored
   gelatin

7 egg yolks, beaten
7 egg whites, beaten until
   stiff
1½ cups heavy cream,
   whipped stiff
½ cup heavy cream
2 Tbs. confectioners sugar
   Finely chopped pecans
   (optional)

Fold waxed paper, 26 inches long, in thirds. With string, tie around 1-quart soufflé dish, to form collar 2 inches high. In top of double boiler, combine Kahlua, brewed coffee, ¾ tsp. coffee granules, confectioners sugar, almond extract, gelatin and egg yolks: mix well. Cook over boiling water (water should not touch bottom of double boiler), stirring occasionally, until mixture thickens and mounds when dropped from spoon. With wire whisk, using an under-and-over motion, fold egg whites and whipped cream into gelatin mixture. Turn mixture into prepared soufflé dish, wineglasses or dessert dishes. Refrigerate until firm—several hours or overnight. Before serving: In Chilled bowl, combine ½ cup heavy cream and 2 Tbs. confectioners sugar; beat together until stiff. Spoon into pastry bag with a number-6 star tip. Sprinkle lightly with coffee granules. If desired, press finely chopped pecans around edge. Makes 8 to 10 servings.

Sierra Snow Cap

Remember Grandma's prune whip? This light, but lavish, dessert from Sun-Sweet® Apricots is a sophisticated version.

1¼ cups Sun-Sweet®
    Apricots
1¼ cups water
 ½ cup sugar
  5 egg whites, unbeaten
 ¼ tsp. salt
  3 to 4 Tbs. brandy (or ¼ tsp.
    almond extract)

Cook apricots in water 10 minutes, until soft. Cool. Drain and measure 1 cup. Chop and combine with sugar, egg whites and salt in top of double boiler. Beat over boiling water with rotary beater until thick enough to hold its shape, about 5 minutes. Remove from heat; gently fold in brandy. Serve warm or cold, garnished with reserved apricots. Makes 4 to 6 servings.

Frosty Orange Stars

Here's the recipe that gives the "how to" for preparing star-shaped orange shells. It's one of Sunkist® growers "most requested."

   Grated peel of 1 Sunkist® Orange
1 peach, nectarine, banana or kiwi, peeled,
   mashed
1 pint vanilla ice cream, softened
2 Sunkist® oranges, cut into 4 star-shaped shells*

* To make 2-star shaped orange shells, cut each orange as follows: Insert tip of paring knife, diagonally, half way between stem and blossom ends. Cut around orange (inserting knife in and pulling out) in a zigzag pattern. Make sure to cut through to center of orange. Give a slight twist to pull apart halves. Carefully ream out juice; drink or reserve for cooking. Scrape shells "clean" with spoon.

In bowl, combine orange peel, peach and ice cream; return to freezer. Scoop frozen ice cream into orange shells. Makes 4 servings.

Variation: Substitute orange sherbet for orange peel, mashed peach and vanilla ice cream.

Plum Cobbler

Do people really make cobblers these days? Of course they do. Requests come into the Karo® test kitchens in a steady stream for this recipe. It was on the label quite some time ago, but word of mouth keeps its reputation going.

¾ cup Karo® Light Corn
    Syrup
1 Tbs. corn starch
½ tsp. ground cinnamon
2 lb. ripe fresh plums,
    pitted, quartered

1¼ cups buttermilk baking
    mix
½ cup finely chopped nuts
    (optional)
⅓ cup milk
¼ cup sugar

Stir together first 3 ingredients; toss with plums. Spoon into 8 × 8 × 2-inch baking dish. Bake in 400°F. oven 15 minutes. Meanwhile, mix remaining ingredients. Beat vigorously 20 strokes. Drop by spoonfuls onto hot plums. Bake 15 to 20 minutes longer. Serves 6.

Butter-Cream Baked Apples

Most people remember these classic Land O Lakes® baked apples as "comforting" food of their childhood. Baked with butter and sugar that turns into a rich sauce when cream is added, they are just as comforting and delicious today.

4 medium baking apples,	1 Tbs. corn starch
cored and not peeled	1 Tbs. cold water
1 cup sugar	½ cup whipping cream
½ cup Land O Lakes® Sweet	
Cream Butter	

Preheat oven to 450°F. Place apples in 1½- or 2-quart round glass baking dish. Sprinkle with sugar; dot with butter. Bake near center of 450°F. oven for 20 to 30 minutes, stirring, basting and turning two times, until apples are fork tender. Meanwhile, combine corn starch and water; add to cream; set aside. Remove apples; stir in cream and corn starch mixture. Return apples to pan. Return to oven for 8 to 10 minutes or until sauce thickens and bubbles all over. Serve apples with sauce spooned over. Makes 4 servings.

Blueberry Chocolate Puffs

Here's a superb, very French, pastry dessert that's as easy to make as it is delectable to eat. From the test kitchens of Pepperidge Farm®.

1 package 17¼-oz
   Pepperidge Farm® Frozen
   Puff Pastry Sheets
1 egg mixed with 1 tsp. water
⅔ cup blueberry jam
3 squares (3 ozs.) semi-sweet
   chocolate
2 Tbs. vegetable shortening

Thaw pastry 20 minutes, then unfold. Roll each square lightly until exactly 10 inches square. Cut each sheet into 25 2-inch rounds. Place rounds on ungreased baking sheets and brush with egg mixture; chill 10 minutes. Bake pastry rounds in preheated 425°F. oven for 12 to 15 minutes or until puffed and golden brown. Transfer to wire racks and cool completely. With a sharp knife, split each puff and spread bottom half with ½ tsp. blueberry jam; replace top half to make a sandwich. Repeat until all puffs are filled. Melt chocolate; add shortening and stir until smooth. Using a spoon drizzle chocolate back and forth over each puff. Let puffs stand until chocolate hardens. Makes 25 puffs.

Homemade Blueberry Jam

2½ cups fresh or dry-pack frozen blueberries
3 cups sugar
⅓ cup orange juice
1 Tbs. lemon juice
½ bottle (3 ozs.) fruit pectin

Wash blueberries. Measure 2½ cups into an enamel or stainless steel pan. Crush blueberries in pan. Add sugar and fruit juices. Mix well. Bring to a full rolling boil and boil hard for one minute, stirring constantly. Remove from heat. Stir in pectin. Seal in hot sterilized jars. Refrigerate. Can be kept for two months. Makes 3 cups 4 6-oz. jars.

Swiss Chocolate Squares

The good cooks at the Parkay® Margarine test kitchens developed this "new" way to mix up a cake back in the 1960's. It's terrific—and quick.

1 cup water
½ cup Parkay® Margarine
1½ 1-oz. squares
    unsweetened chocolate
2 cups flour
2 cups sugar
2 eggs
½ cup dairy sour cream
1 tsp. baking soda

½ tsp. salt
½ cup Parkay® Margarine
6 Tbs. milk
1½ 1-oz. squares
    unsweetened chocolate
4½ cups sifted confectioners
    sugar
1 tsp. vanilla
½ cup chopped nuts

Combine water, margarine and chocolate in saucepan; bring to boil. Remove from heat. Stir in combined flour and sugar. Add eggs, sour cream, baking soda and salt; mix well. Pour into greased and floured 15½ × 10½-inch jelly roll pan. Bake at 375°F. 20 to 25 minutes. Combine margarine, milk and chocolate in saucepan; bring to boil. Remove from heat. Add sugar; beat until smooth. Stir in vanilla. Frost cake while warm; sprinkle with nuts. Cool; cut into squares. Makes about 24 squares.

Cantaloupe Sherbet

A 1970's "summertime, and the living is easy" time dessert from Karo®. It's one of the simplest of recipes to put together, and it's light, airy and refreshing.

1 envelope unflavored gelatin
½ cup milk
3 cups cubed cantaloupe
1 cup Karo® Light Corn Syrup

In small saucepan sprinkle gelatin over milk. Stir over low heat until dissolved. Place in blender container with cantaloupe and corn syrup; cover. Blend on high speed 30 seconds. Pour into 9 × 9 × 2-inch baking pan. Cover; freeze overnight. Soften slightly at room temperature, about 10 to 15 minutes. Spoon into large bowl; with mixer at low speed, beat until smooth, but not melted. Pour into 4-cup mold or freezer container. Cover; freeze about 4 hours or until firm. Unmold or soften at room temperature for easier scooping. Makes about 4 cups.

Blueberry Sherbet: Follow basic recipe. Use 3 cups whole blueberries; omit cantaloupe. Makes about 3½ cups.

Honeydew Sherbet: Follow basic recipe. Use 3 cups cubed honeydew melon; omit cantaloupe. Makes about 4 cups.

Nectarine or Peach Sherbet: Follow basic recipe. Use 3 cups cubed nectarines or peaches and 1 Tbs. lemon juice; omit cantaloupe. Makes about 4 cups.

Papaya Sherbet: Follow basic recipe. Use 3 cups cubed papaya and 1 Tbs. lemon juice; omit cantaloupe. Makes about 4 cups.

Pineapple Sherbet: Follow basic recipe. Use 3 cups cubed pineapple; omit cantaloupe. Makes about 4 cups.

Strawberry Sherbet: Follow basic recipe. Use 3 cups whole strawberries; omit cantaloupe. Makes about 3½ cups.

Watermelon Sherbet: Follow basic recipe. Use 3 cups cubed watermelon; omit cantaloupe. Makes about 4 cups.

Brandied Raspberry Bavarian

**For many years this was a favorite recipe on the Dole®
Crushed Pineapple label. It was so popular it was reprinted
in a booklet and used in national advertisements, too.**

1 1-lb., 4-oz. can Dole®
Crushed Pineapple in
Juice
2 6-oz. packages raspberry
gelatin
3 cups boiling water

2 cups cold water
1 tsp. grated lemon peel
½ cup brandy
½ pint whipping cream
2 Tbs. sugar

Drain pineapple reserving all juice. Dissolve gelatin in boiling water. Stir in reserved pineapple juice, cold water, lemon peel and brandy. Chill to consistency of unbeaten egg white. Whip cream with sugar. Fold into thickened gelatin along with drained pineapple. Pour into Bundt pan. Chill overnight. Makes 10 servings.

Broken Window Glass Cake

**The way food looks is second only to the way it tastes. In the
"sweet ending" class, one seldom comes by a dessert that
has such style and appeal as this elegant gelatin-cake combination. It comes from *The New Joys of Jello-O*® book, first
printed in 1973.**

1 3-oz. package Jell-O®
  Brand Orange Flavor
  Gelatin
1 3-oz. package Jell-O®
  Brand Cherry Flavor
  Gelatin
1 3 oz. package Jell-O®
  Brand Lime Flavor
  Gelatin
3 cups boiling water
1½ cups cold water
1½ cups graham cracker
  crumbs

⅓ cup butter or margarine,
  melted
1 3-oz. package Jell-O®
  Brand Lemon Flavor
  Gelatin
¼ cup sugar
1 cup boiling water
½ cup canned pineapple
  juice
1 8-oz. container Birds Eye®
  Cool Whip Non-Dairy
  Whipped Topping,
  thawed

Prepare the orange, cherry and lime gelatins separately, dissolving each in 1 cup boiling water and adding ½ cup of the cold water. Pour each flavor into separate 8-inch square pan. Chill until firm, at least 3 hours or overnight. Cut into ½-inch cubes. Mix crumbs with butter. Set aside about ¼ cup for garnish, if desired, and press remaining crumb mixture evenly over bottom and up sides to within 1 inch from top of 9-inch springform or tube pan. Chill. Dissolve lemon gelatin and sugar in 1 cup boiling water; add pineapple juice. Chill until slightly thickened. Blend in whipped topping. Fold in gelatin cubes. Spoon into crumb-lined pan. Chill overnight or until firm. Just before serving, run a spatula around sides of pan; then gently remove sides. Garnish with reserved crumbs or with additional whipped topping and flaked coconut, tinted, if desired. Makes 12 to 16 servings.

Mai-Tai Mold

The recipe for this beautiful dessert appeared in Dole® Pineapple advertising some years ago and customers still

ask for it. I depart from the last line directions; I unmold it, but serve the whipped cream on the side. It's just too pretty to cover when it first comes to the table.

1 1-lb., 4-oz. can Dole® Pineapple Chunks in Juice
2 6-oz. packages orange gelatin
3 cups boiling water
2 cups cold water
½ cup dark rum or orange juice

3 large mint sprigs
12 Maraschino cherries
1 orange, peeled and sectioned
Sweetened whipped cream

Drain pineapple, reserving all juice. Dissolve gelatin in boiling water. Stir in cold water and rum. Arrange mint sprigs, 3 or 4 cherries and several pineapple chunks in bottom of Bundt pan. Pour in ½ cup gelatin mixture. Chill firm. Chill remaining gelatin to consistency of unbeaten egg white. Fold in pineapple, cherries and orange sections. Pour over mint sprigs. Chill firm overnight. Unmold and top with whipped cream to serve. Makes 8 to 10 servings.

Crème de Menthe Crown

Here's a superb extra-easy dessert to end dinner in style. It is from the Dole® Pineapple people—a recipe worth keeping for special occasions and special people.

1 1-lb., 4-oz. can Dole® Sliced Pineapple
2 6-oz. packages lime gelatin
3 cups boiling water

1½ cups cold water
6 Tbs. Crème de Menthe
½ pint whipping cream
¼ cup sugar
1 tsp. vanilla

Drain pineapple, reserving all syrup. Dissolve gelatin in boiling water. Stir in pineapple syrup, cold water and Crème de Menthe. Pour 1 cup mixture into bottom of Bundt pan. Arrange 3 slices of pineapple, cut in halves, in gelatin mixture in bottom of Bundt pan. Chill firm. Cut through gelatin with spatula at pan ridges. Stand remaining slices in ridges. Chill remainder to consistency of unbeaten egg white. Whip cream with sugar and vanilla until stiff. Fold into thickened gelatin mixture. Spoon into Bundt pan between pineapple slices and over top. Chill until firm overnight. Makes 10 servings.

Pineapple Crème Brûlée

Sensationally rich and flavorful but one of the simplest of all desserts to make. An elegant friend served it not too long ago at one of her elegant dinner parties. She was nice enough to tell me where to find the recipe: on the inside label of Coco Casa® Piña Colada mix.

3 cups heavy cream	6 egg yolks
1 2-inch piece vanilla bean (split lengthwise) or 2 tsps. vanilla extract	1 cup Coco Casa® Piña Colada Mix
2 tsps. corn starch	2 Tbs. cognac or brandy
	2 Tbs. dark brown sugar

In a saucepan, combine heavy cream and vanilla; heat until scalded. In a bowl, beat egg yolks and corn starch until smooth. Slowly stir in scalded cream, Piña Colada mix and liquor. Strain mixture into a baking dish. Place dish in a pan containing 1 inch hot water. Bake at 325°F. for 35 to 40 minutes or until set. Chill several hours or overnight. Before serving, sprinkle surface with brown sugar. Place dish over ice in a baking pan. Place under a preheated broiler until sugar is melted, about 5 minutes. Serve immediately. Serves 6 to 8.

Basic Dannon Yogurt Dessert

This has become a classic and part of our true American cuisine.

2 cups Dannon® Plain Yogurt
½ cup sugar
2 Tbs. lemon juice
3 Tbs. orange liqueur
1 pint softened vanilla ice cream

Mix sugar, lemon juice, orange liqueur and Dannon® Plain Yogurt. Stir softened vanilla ice cream and fold into other ingredients. Serves about 4 people.

Variations:

Mold in salad mold and freeze. Unmold on serving plate and surround with fresh strawberries, peaches, blueberries, raspberries, grapes, etc.

Alternate layers in a glass bowl: grapes, raspberries, blueberries, melon balls and Basic Dannon® Yogurt Dessert.

Mix any type of fruit and Basic Dannon® Yogurt Dessert and use as a filling for crêpes.

Mix any type of fruit and Basic Dannon® Yogurt Dessert and spoon into pie crust and freeze until set.

9.

Special Sweets
and Treats

You know our best memories are not only from great moments, but also from the many small events in our lives. It's true. Since completing the very first collection of "Best Recipes" over three years ago, I have received dozens upon dozens of "clipped" recipes, most of them tattered, stained and old, from people in just about every one of the United States. With each one there was always a note that went something like this: "My mother (or aunt or older sister) always made these wonderful cookies (or candy) at holiday time (or on my birthday, or on some other special occasion), and I remember . . . "

Isn't it wonderful that something so simple, so innocent, could bring such a response?

No matter how action-filled your life may be, how hurried or harried, do find the small time it takes to whip up one or two of the recipes to follow. Fond memories don't always have to be old and dusty to be enjoyed.

The cookies and candies here are truly memorable. Just try them and see. Make a platter of tart-sweet apricot bars to share with friends over a pot of freshly brewed coffee or whip up a batch of creamy smooth penuche; just what's needed to enjoy the late, late movie on TV—and don't feel guilty about it, even if you are carefully watching your weight. Nutritionists, doctors, even weight-loss experts, have finally come to the happy conclusion that spartan diets don't work; the only way to lose unwanted pounds *permanently* is to step up activities, eat a sensible diet that is nutritionally balanced, cut down on the amount you eat, but *don't cut out* all the food you enjoy. We all need that sweet part of our lives, if not every day at least now and then for a special treat.

Each and every one of the recipes here are easy to make and of course failproof. Our test-kitchen experts have seen to that. They are thrifty, too, but they are also much more. Although the ingredients used are the usual butter and sugar, eggs, flour, spice and such, the end results are rather magical! Like millions of other people, once you have tasted them you'll remember their special goodness, the pleasure they gave, the good times shared, the picnics, the parties and special days—in fact—whenever they were part of the good food and fun.

Peanut Butter Kisses

A classic from the Skippy® Peanut Butter label; easy to make, inexpensive and they love 'em.

2 egg whites
⅛ tsp. cream of tartar
⅔ cup sugar
½ cup Skippy® Creamy or Super Chunk
Peanut Butter

In small bowl with mixer at high speed beat egg whites and cream of tartar until mixture holds stiff peaks when beater is raised. Add sugar, 1 Tbs. at a time, beating well after each addition. Continue beating until mixture holds very stiff peaks when beater is raised. Lightly fold in peanut butter just until mixed. Drop by teaspoonfuls onto greased cookie sheet. Bake in 300°F. oven 25 minutes or until lightly browned. Remove from cookie sheet immediately. Makes about 3 dozen cookies.

Brown-Eyed Susans

A rich, chocolate-topped cookie with almond "eyes"—the popularity of this Parkay® "classic" dates from the 1940's and has not diminished with passing time.

1 cup Parkay® Margarine
¼ cup sugar
½ tsp. almond extract
2 cups flour
½ tsp. salt
Chocolate Frosting (below)
Whole almonds

Cream margarine and sugar until light and fluffy. Blend in extract. Add flour and salt; mix well. Shape rounded teaspoonfuls of dough into balls. Place on ungreased cookie sheet; flatten slightly. Bake at 375°F., 10 to 12 minutes. Cool. Frost with Chocolate Frosting; top with almonds. Makes approximately 5 dozen.

Chocolate Frosting

1 cup confectioners sugar, sifted
2 Tbs. cocoa
1 Tbs. hot water
½ tsp. vanilla

Combine sugar and cocoa. Add water and vanilla and mix well.

Butter Pecan Turtle Cookies

An irresistibly good cookie made easy by the talented cooks at the Land O Lakes® test kitchens.

Crust
2 cups all-purpose flour
1 cup firmly packed brown sugar
½ cup Land O Lakes® Sweet Cream Butter, softened
1 cup whole pecan halves (not chopped)

Preheat oven to 350°F. In 3-quart mixer bowl combine crust ingredients. Mix at medium .speed, scraping sides of bowl often, until well mixed and particles are fine (2 to 3 minutes). Pat firmly into ungreased 13 × 9 × 2-inch pan. Sprinkle pecans evenly over unbaked crust. Prepare caramel layer; pour evenly over pecans and crust. Bake near center of 350°F. oven for 18 to 22 minutes or until entire caramel layer is bubbly and crust is light golden brown. Remove from oven. Immediately sprinkle with chips. Allow chips to melt slightly (2 to 3 minutes). Slightly swirl chips as they melt; leave some whole for a marbled effect. Do not spread chips. Cool completely; cut into bars. Makes 3 to 4 dozen bars.

Caramel Layer
⅔ cup Land O Lakes® Sweet Cream Butter
½ cup firmly packed brown sugar
1 cup milk-chocolate chips

Caramel Layer: In heavy 1-quart saucepan combine butter and brown sugar. Cook over medium heat, stirring constantly, until entire surface of mixture begins to boil. Boil ½ to 1 minute, stirring constantly.

Chewy Walnut Squares

We've been making these cookies from the Diamond® Walnut Growers every Christmas as far back as I can remember. "They are so good they deserve to be put in your book" wrote several different fans.

1 egg, unbeaten
1 cup brown sugar, packed
1 tsp. vanilla
½ cup sifted all-purpose
    flour

¼ tsp. baking soda
¼ tsp. salt
1 cup coarsely chopped
    Diamond® Walnuts

Grease an 8-inch square pan. Stir together the egg, brown sugar and vanilla. Quickly stir in flour, baking soda and salt. Add Walnuts. Spread in pan and bake at 350°F. for 18 to 20 minutes. (Cookies should be soft in center when taken from oven.) Leave in pan; cut into 2-inch squares. Makes 16 squares.

Butterscotch Brownies

These old-fashioned cookies from Nestlé® have been making butterscotch fanciers happy for a very long time.

2 cups *unsifted* flour
2 tsps. baking powder
1½ tsps. salt
One 12-oz. package (2 cups) Nestlé® Butterscotch Morsels

½ cup butter
2 cups firmly packed brown sugar
4 eggs
1 tsp. vanilla extract
1 cup chopped nuts

Preheat oven to 350°F. In small bowl, combine flour, baking powder and salt; set aside. Melt over hot (not boiling) water, Nestlé® Butterscotch Morsels and butter; remove from heat and transfer to large bowl. Stir in brown sugar. Cool 5 minutes. Beat in eggs and vanilla extract. Blend in flour mixture. Stir in nuts. Spread evenly into greased 15 × 10 × 1-inch baking pan. Bake at 350°F. for 30 minutes. Cool. Cut into 2-inch squares. Makes 35 2-inch squares.

Note: For one 6-oz. package, recipe may be divided in half. Spread into greased 13 × 9 × 2-inch baking pan. Bake for 25 to 30 minutes. Makes 24 2-inch squares.

"Philly" Sprites

A cream cheese version of spritz and a Kraft® classic.

1 cup margarine
1 8-oz. package Philadelphia® Brand Cream Cheese

⅔ cup sugar
1 tsp. vanilla
2 cups flour
Dash of salt

Combine margarine, softened Cream Cheese and sugar, mixing until well blended. Blend in vanilla. Add flour and salt; mix well. Chill. Force dough through cookie press onto ungreased cookie sheet. Bake at 400°F., 8 to 10 minutes. Makes approximately 8 dozen.

Spritz Cookies

These buttery rich "no chill" cookies from the Land O Lakes® Sweet Cream Butter carton have been a favorite for a generation.

1 cup Land O Lakes® Sweet Cream Butter, softened
⅔ cup sugar
1 egg

2 tsp. vanilla or almond or lemon flavoring
2¼ cups all-purpose flour
½ tsp. salt

Preheat oven to 400°F. In 3-quart mixer bowl combine butter, sugar, egg and flavoring. Beat at medium speed, scraping sides of bowl often, until light and fluffy. Reduce to low speed (or by hand); stir in flour and salt until well combined. Dough can be divided and tinted if desired. If dough is too soft, chill for easier handling. Force dough through a cookie press onto ungreased baking sheet. Decorate with colored sugar or cinnamon candies, etc. Bake near center of 400°F. oven for 8 to 14 minutes or until cookies are light golden around edges. Makes 6 dozen cookies.

Tip: For green or pink cookies, add 3 to 4 drops green or red food coloring.

Cross-Country Oatmeal Cookies

**Americans have been munching these old-fashioned oatmeal cookies since they were first introduced by Mazola®
in the mid 1930's, but the updated version is as modern as
tomorrow. They are low in fat and have only a moderate
amount of cholesterol, sugar and salt.**

¾ cup Mazola® Corn Oil
1 cup firmly packed brown
   sugar
2 eggs
1 tsp. vanilla
1½ cups unsifted flour

1 cup quick-cooking oats
1½ tsps. baking powder
½ tsp. salt
½ tsp. ground cinnamon
½ cup coarsely chopped
   nuts

In large bowl with mixer at medium speed beat corn oil,
sugar, eggs and vanilla until thick. Add flour, oats, baking powder, salt and cinnamon. Beat at low speed until
blended. Stir in nuts. Drop by level tablespoonfuls 2
inches apart on greased cookie sheet. Bake in 350°F. oven
12 to 15 minutes or until browned. Makes about 3½
dozen.

Oatmeal Scotchies

**Oatmeal, brown sugar and Nestle® Butterscotch Morsels
have made these moist and rich cookies a favorite since the
1950's.**

2 cups *unsifted* flour
2 tsps. baking powder
1 tsp. baking soda
1 tsp. salt
1 cup butter, softened
1½ cups firmly packed
   brown sugar
2 eggs

1 Tbs. water
1½ cups quick oats, un-
   cooked
One 12-oz. package (2
   cups) Nestlé®
   Butterscotch Morsels
½ tsp. orange extract

Preheat oven to 375°F. In small bowl, combine flour, baking powder, baking soda and salt; set aside. In large bowl, combine butter, brown sugar, eggs and water; beat until creamy. Gradually add flour mixture. Stir in oats, Nestlé® Butterscotch Morsels and orange extract. Drop by slightly rounded tablespoonfuls onto greased cookie sheets. Bake at 375°F. for 10 to 12 minutes. Makes 4 dozen 3-inch cookies.

Double Chocolate Oatmeal Cookies

A top-request recipe and a particular favorite with the Betty Crocker® staff. Made to order for after-school treats.

1½ cups sugar
1 cup margarine or butter, softened
1 egg
¼ cup water
1 tsp. vanilla
1¼ cups Gold Medal® All-Purpose Flour*

⅓ cup cocoa
½ tsp. baking soda
½ tsp. salt
3 cups quick-cooking oats
1 6-oz. package semi-sweet chocolate chips

Heat oven to 350°F. Mix sugar, margarine, egg, water and vanilla. Stir in remaining ingredients. Drop dough

* If using self-rising flour, omit baking soda and salt.

by rounded teaspoonfuls about 2 inches apart onto ungreased cookie sheet. Bake until almost no indentation remains when touched, 10 to 12 minutes. Immediately remove from cookie sheet. About 5½ dozen cookies.

Note: Unbleached flour can be used in this recipe.

Snowy Apricot Bars

An old-fashioned favorite from Bisquick®; these rich fruit and nut bars often appear at showers, weddings and holiday buffets.

1 6-oz. package dried apricots (1⅓ cups)
½ cup firm margarine or butter
½ cup granulated sugar
2½ cups Bisquick® Baking Mix
2 cups packed brown sugar

4 eggs, beaten
⅔ cup Bisquick® Baking Mix
1 tsp. vanilla
1 cup chopped nuts
Powdered sugar

Place apricots in 2-quart saucepan; add enough water to cover. Heat to boiling; reduce heat. Simmer uncovered 10 minutes; drain. Cool; chop and reserve. Heat oven to 350°F. Cut margarine into granulated sugar and 2½ cups Baking Mix until crumbly. Pat in ungreased jelly roll pan, 15½ × 1-inch. Bake 10 minutes. Beat brown sugar and eggs. Stir in apricots, ⅔ cup Baking Mix, the vanilla and nuts. Spread over baked layer. Bake 30 minutes longer. Cool completely; cut into bars, about 2 × 1 inches each. Roll in powdered sugar. Makes 75 cookies.

Speedy Little Devils

A very "early on" creamy-center bar cookie from the label of a Duncan Hines® Cake Mix box; printed way back when most people thought cake mixes only made cakes. Love these cookies; my only complaint is how in heaven's name can anyone follow the last line of the directions in the recipe, "Serve one piece at a time?" You just can't do that at my house.

1 package Duncan Hines® II Devil's Food
   Cake Mix
1 stick butter or margarine, melted
¾ cup creamy peanut butter
1 7 to 7½-oz. jar marshmallow creme

Combine melted butter and dry Cake Mix (let butter cool down a couple of minutes before adding to dry mix. Mixture should be crumbly. If butter is too hot, the result will be a sticky mass rather than a crumbly mixture.) Reserve 1½ cups of this mixture for topping. Pat remaining crumb mixture into an ungreased 13 × 9 × 2-inch pan. Combine peanut butter and marshmallow creme and spread evenly over the crumb mixture in the pan. Crumble the reserved 1½ cups of cake mixture over the peanut butter/marshmallow creme layer. Bake 20 minutes at 350°F. Let cool, cut into bars, and serve one piece at a time. Makes 3 dozen 1¼-inch bars.

Baby Ruth Cookies

Remember how you loved them? The recipe, from a booklet printed in the early 1950's, has been one of the "most requested" at the Standard Brands' kitchens for over 25 years. Due to its popularity it was reprinted on the package in the late 1970's. **People who remember making them for their children now want a reprint of the recipe for their grandchildren.**

1¼ cups unsifted flour
½ tsp. baking soda
½ tsp. salt
½ cup (1 stick) Blue Bonnet
    Margarine

¾ cup sugar
1 egg
½ tsp. vanilla
1 cup chopped Curtiss®
    Baby Ruth Candy Bars

Sift together flour, baking soda and salt; set aside. Cream together Blue Bonnet® Margarine and sugar until light and fluffy. Beat in egg and vanilla. Stir in Curtiss® Baby Ruths and dry ingredients until well blended. Chill for 30 minutes. Drop dough by ½-teaspoonfuls onto greased baking sheets. Bake at 350°F. for 10 to 12 minutes, or until done. Remove from sheets and cool on wire racks.

Choco-Almond Confections

This positively elegant "very adult" confection is from Blue Diamond.®

1¼ cups Blue Diamond®
    Chopped Natural
    Almonds, toasted
3 1-oz. squares milk
    chocolate
½ cup orange juice

½ cup granulated sugar
3 cups crushed lemon,
    orange or vanilla wafers
2 Tbs. Curacao or orange
    juice

In blender or food processor, finely grind ¼ cup of the almonds; set aside. Combine chocolate with orange juice and sugar in saucepan. Cook over medium heat, stirring constantly until sugar is dissolved and chocolate is melted. Remove from heat and mix in crushed wafers, Curacao and the chopped almonds. Chill mixture at least one hour. Form into small balls; roll in the ground almonds. Refrigerate in air-tight container for several days for best flavor to develop. Makes about 3 dozen.

Applesauce Bars

Rich, moist and spicy good. The entire family will love these cookies from Stokely– Van Camp.®

2½ cups all-purpose flour
1 cup sugar
¼ tsp. baking powder
1½ tsps. baking soda
1½ tsps. salt
¾ tsp. cinnamon
½ tsp. cloves
½ tsp. allspice
½ cup vegetable
   shortening, at room
   temperature
½ cup water
1 16½-oz. can Stokely's
   Finest® Applesauce
1 egg
½ cup chopped nuts
1 cup chopped raisins
   Caramel Frosting
   (below)

Preheat oven to 350°F. Grease and flour 15 × 10 × 1-inch jelly-roll pan. Sift all dry ingredients into a large mixing bowl. Add shortening, water, applesauce and egg. Beat 4 minutes with electric mixer on medium speed. Gently fold in nuts and raisins. Pour into prepared pan and bake 30 minutes. Cool in pan. Frost cake in pan and cut into bars. Makes 48 bars.

Caramel Frosting

¼ cup butter or margarine
½ cup firmly packed brown sugar
3 Tbs. milk
   About 1½ cups sifted confectioners sugar

Melt butter, add brown sugar; boil for 1 minute, stirring constantly. Cool slightly. Stir in milk. Gradually add confectioners sugar and beat until of spreading consistency.

Yugoslav Kifle
(Filled Butterhorn Cookie)

A sweet walnut-meringue cookie made with a yeast dough. Your mother may have called them Butterhorns and found the recipe on a Fleischmann's® Yeast label. If she made them you'll remember; once tried they are never forgotten.

½ cup dairy sour cream
1 Tbs. boiling water
1 package Fleischmann's® Active Dry Yeast
½ cup (1 stick) Fleischmann's® Margarine, softened
1¾ to 2¼ cups unsifted flour
2 egg yolks (at room temperature)

1 cup finely chopped Planters® Walnuts
½ cup sugar
1 tsp. vanilla extract
2 egg whites, stiffly beaten
Confectioners sugar
Melted Fleischmann's® Margarine

Combine sour cream and boiling water; mix well. Stir in undissolved Fleischmann's® Active Dry Yeast; let stand 3 minutes. Stir until yeast is completely dissolved; set aside. Place softened Fleischmann's® Margarine and ½ cup flour in small bowl. Add sour cream mixture and beat 1 minute at low speed of electric mixer, scraping bowl occasionally. Add egg yolks and ¼ cup flour; beat at medium speed 1 minute, scraping bowl occasionally. Stir in enough additional flour to make a soft dough. Turn out onto lightly floured board; knead 8 to 10 minutes. (Dough will not be smooth.) Divide dough into 3 equal pieces. Wrap in wax paper. Chill at least 2 hours or up to

5 days. When ready to shape, combine Planters® Walnuts, sugar and vanilla extract. Fold in stiffly beaten egg whites. On a board dusted with confectioners sugar, roll each piece of dough into a 10-inch circle; cut each into 8 pie-shaped wedges. Top wide edge of each wedge with about 1 Tbs. nut filling mixture. Roll up from wide end to point. Place on greased baking sheets, with points underneath. Brush with melted Fleischmann's® Margarine. Bake at 375°F. for 20 minutes, or until golden brown. Remove from baking sheets and place on wire racks to cool. Immediately sprinkle with confectioners sugar if desired. Makes 2 dozen cookies.

Crunchy Fudge Sandwiches

No one knows how many millions of cupfuls of Kellogg's® Rice Krispies® have been used for this sensational recipe.

One 6-oz. package
(1 cup) butterscotch-
flavored morsels
½ cup peanut butter
4 cups Kellogg's® Rice
Krispies® Cereal
One 6-oz. package (1 cup)
semi-sweet chocolate
morsels

½ cup sifted confectioners
sugar
2 Tbs. margarine or butter,
softened
1 Tbs. water

In large saucepan, melt butterscotch-flavored morsels and peanut butter over very low heat, stirring constantly until smooth. Stir in Cereal. Press half the mixture in a buttered 8 × 8 × 2-inch pan. Chill. Set remaining mixture aside. Melt over hot (not boiling) water semi-sweet morsels, sugar, margarine and water, stirring constantly until smooth. Spread over chilled Cereal mixture. Spread remaining Cereal mixture evenly over top. Press in gently. Chill until firm (1 hour). Makes 25 squares, 1½ × 1½ inches each.

Pecan Turtles

Here's a very special and extremely popular recipe for Turtles, made with Planters® Pecans. Great for special occasions, for gift giving or just for you.

½ cup (1 stick) Blue
  Bonnet® Margarine
1 cup firmly packed light
  brown sugar
  Dash salt
½ cup light corn syrup
⅔ cup sweetened
  condensed milk

1½ cups Planters® Pecan
  Pieces
½ tsp. vanilla extract
1 6-oz. package semi-
  sweet chocolate
  morsels, melted

Melt Blue Bonnet® Margarine over medium heat in a medium saucepan. Stir in brown sugar and salt. Mix in corn syrup and sweetened condensed milk. Cook, stirring occasionally, to 245°F. (firm-ball stage), about 15 to 20 minutes. Remove from heat; stir in Planters® Pecan Pieces and vanilla. Drop by tablespoonfuls onto greased baking sheets. When cooled and firm, dip into melted chocolate to coat top. Return to greased baking sheet and cool until chocolate is set. Store candies in a closed container in a cool place.

Crunchy Mounds

It's impossible to fail with this crunchy crisp and delicious candy from Skippy® Peanut Butter. You don't even need a candy thermometer. A teenage favorite to make and to eat.

1 6-oz. package semi-sweet chocolate pieces
¼ cup Skippy® Creamy or Super Chunk Peanut
   Butter
2⅓ cups corn flakes
⅓ cup dry-roated peanuts

In 1-quart saucepan stir together chocolate pieces and peanut butter. Cook over low heat until melted. Stir in corn flakes and nuts. Drop by teaspoonfuls onto waxed paper. Cool 15 to 20 minutes or until set. Makes about 32 1½-inch cookies.

Creamy-Sure Fudge

A number of different people sent me this "can't fail" fudge recipe from Diamond® Walnuts. They voted it "best of the best."

1⅓ cups granulated sugar
⅔ cup (1 small can)
   undiluted evaporated
   milk
¼ cup butter
1 jar regular size
   (approximately 7 ozs.)
   marshmallow creme, or
   16 large marshmallows,
   quartered

¼ tsp. salt
1 12-oz. package (2 cups)
   semi-sweet chocolate
   pieces
1 tsp. vanilla
1 cup coarsely chopped
   Diamond® Walnuts

Combine sugar, undiluted milk, butter, marshmallow creme or marshmallows and salt in 2-quart saucepan. Cook, stirring constantly, until mixture has boiled for exactly 5 minutes. Remove from heat; add chocolate pieces and vanilla and stir until chocolate is melted. Stir in walnuts. Turn into buttered 8-inch square pan. Let stand until firm, then cut into squares. Makes about 2½ lbs. candy.

Country Club Two-Story Fudge

Some inspired candy aficionado at the Hershey® test kitchens came up with this very festive fudge variation in the early 1940's.

First Story:

2½ cups granulated sugar
1 cup milk
3 squares Hershey®'s Baking Chocolate

1 Tbs. light corn syrup
2 Tbs. butter
1 tsp. vanilla
½ cup chopped nutmeats

Combine sugar, milk, Baking Chocolate broken into small pieces, and the corn syrup in a heavy saucepan (3-quart). Place over medium heat and stir gently till Baking Chocolate is melted, then cook with very little stirring to soft-ball stage (234°F.). Remove from the fire; add butter and vanilla. Cool, undisturbed, to lukewarm (110°F.). Beat vigorously until fudge thickens and starts to lose its gloss; add nuts and quickly pour into a buttered 9 × 9 × 1¾-inch pan. Set aside to cool.

Second Story:

2½ cups granulated sugar
½ cup light cream
½ cup milk
¼ tsp. salt
1 Tbs. light corn syrup

2 Tbs. butter
1 tsp. vanilla
⅓ cupful chopped glâcé cherries

Butter sides of a heavy saucepan (2-quart). In it combine sugar, cream, milk, salt and corn syrup. Place over medium heat, and stir until sugar is dissolved, then cook to soft-ball stage (236°F.). Remove from fire; add butter and vanilla. Cool, undisturbed, to lukewarm (110°F.). Beat vigorously until mixture becomes very thick and starts to lose its gloss. Quickly stir in glâcé cherries, and pour over the dark fudge, smoothing the surface with a knife. Cut into squares while still warm. Makes 4 dozen pieces.

Chocolate Seafoam

Light and airy, but rich as only good chocolate candy can be; a Hershey® Town classic.

2 cups light brown sugar, packed
¾ cup cold water
½ cup (5½-oz. can) Hershey®'s Chocolate Flavored Syrup

2 egg whites
1 tsp. vanilla
1 square Hershey®'s Baking Chocolate, melted
½ cup nutmeats

Mix together sugar, water and Chocolate Syrup in a heavy saucepan (3-quart). Cook over medium heat, stirring constantly, till sugar dissolves and mixture boils. Then cook to hard-ball stage (250°F.) without stirring. Remove pan from heat. Immediately beat egg whites till stiff. Pour hot syrup in a thin stream over beaten egg whites, beating constantly at high speed on mixer. Continue beating till mixture forms peaks when dropped from spoon, about 10 minutes. Quickly stir in vanilla and melted baking chocolate by hand. Blend in nutmeats. Drop by teaspoonfuls onto waxed paper. Cool. Makes 3 to 4 dozen pieces.

Crispy Confections

Quick and delicious—an all-time Kraft® favorite.

49 Kraft® caramels (14-oz. bag)
3 Tbs. water
2 cups crisp rice cereal
2 cups corn flakes
1 4-oz. package shredded coconut

Melt caramels with water in saucepan over low heat. Stir frequently until sauce is smooth. Pour over combined cereals and coconut; toss until well coated. Drop rounded tablespoonfuls onto greased cookie sheet; let stand until firm. Makes 4 dozen.

HOMEMADE ALMOND CANDIES

A perfect ending to a little supper party might be this assortment of fine homemade candy from Blue Diamond® Almonds and the California Almond Growers Exchange. All three come from their permanent files of all-time favorite classics.

Almond Brittle

2 cups sugar
⅓ cup light corn syrup
⅔ cup cold water
¼ cup butter or margarine

1 tsp. vanilla
½ tsp. baking soda
1½ cups diced roasted almonds

Combine sugar, syrup, water and butter, and cook and stir until sugar is dissolved. Continue cooking without stirring to 300°F. or when syrup separates into hard brittle threads when dropped into cold water. Remove from heat and stir in vanilla, soda and almonds. Pour onto greased cookie sheet. When slightly cooled, pull edges to make a thin sheet. When thoroughly cold, break into pieces. Makes about 1½ lbs. candy.

Almond Penuche

3 cups brown sugar, packed
⅛ tsp. salt
1 cup milk
2 Tbs. light corn syrup

2 Tbs. butter or margarine
1 tsp. vanilla
1 cup toasted blanched slivered almonds

In saucepan combine sugar, salt, milk and syrup. Cook over low heat, stirring constantly until sugar is dissolved. Boil gently, stirring often to 235°F., or until a little mixture forms a soft ball in cold water. Remove from heat. Add butter and cool without stirring. Add vanilla. Beat until creamy and no longer shiny. Stir in almonds and pour into buttered 8-inch square pan. Cool and cut into squares. Makes 36 squares.

Fruit-Nut Balls

1 cup golden seedless
  raisins
1 cup dried apricots
  Water
1 cup whole natural
  almonds

½ cup shredded coconut,
  toasted
1 to 2 Tbs. honey
  Powdered sugar

Combine raisins and apricots in saucepan with water to partially cover. Simmer, covered, 5 minutes. Drain. Put fruits and almonds through food chopper, using medium blade. Add coconut and honey and mix thoroughly. Shape into small balls. Roll in powdered sugar. Makes about 18 balls.

Index

About the Author

Ceil Dyer is the author of numerous best-selling cookbooks, including *Wok Cookery* and *Carter Family Favorites Cookbook* in addition to McGraw-Hill's *Best Recipes from the Backs of Boxes, Bottles, Cans and Jars* and *More Recipes from the Backs of Boxes, Bottles, Cans and Jars*, both of which have been selected by the Cookbook Guild.